"*Seven Pillars of Wisdom*"

The Art

of One-Name Studies

Introduction: Carrying out a One-Name Study

1 — Data collection

2 — Analysis

3 — Synthesis

4 — Publicising your study

5 — Responding to enquiries

6 — Publication of results

7 — Preserving your study

Appendix: A One-Name Study Plan

April 2012

Table of Contents

0. Introduction to the Art of One-Name Studies 5
0.1 Carrying out a one-name study 5
0.1.1 Definition of a one-name study 5
0.1.2 Hints and tips 6
0.2 The Guild of One-Name Studies 8
0.2.1 Guild membership 8
0.2.2 How the Guild can help your one-name study 9
0.2.2.1 Guild services and facilities 9
0.3 Using a computer for one-name studies 11
0.3.1 Computer requirements 11
0.3.2 Choice of operating system 11
0.3.3 Choice of email systems 12
0.3.3.1 Using your Guild email alias 12
0.3.4 Choice of internet browser 12
0.3.5 Choice of family-tree software 13
0.3.6 Spreadsheets for One-Name Studies 14
0.3.6.1 Spreadsheets for birth, marriage and death (BMD) indexes 15
0.4 The art of searching 16
0.4.1 Useful programs 16

1. Data collection 18
1.1 Starting to collect data 19
1.1.1 Collecting documentary data 19
1.1.2 Collecting genetic data 20
1.1.3 Collecting data from living name-bearers 20
1.1.4 Data collection summary 20
1.2 Sources of documentary data 20
1.2.1 Vital data from the LDS (IGI, VRI, FamilySearch) 21
1.2.1.1 International Genealogical Index 21
1.2.1.2 Vital Records Indexes 21
1.2.1.3 Obtaining copies of documents through the LDS 22
1.2.2 UK Vital Data Sources 22
1.2.2.1 England and Wales – the GRO 22
1.2.2.2 Scotland – GROS 24
1.2.2.3 Northern Ireland – GRONI 24
1.2.3 Vital data for other countries 24
1.2.4 Other sources of vital data 24
1.2.5 Biographical and residential data 25
1.2.5.1 Web search engines 25
1.2.5.2 Book Indexes 27
1.2.5.3 Indexes of Patents 28
1.2.5.4 Reports of Case Law 28
1.2.5.5 Biographical Indexes 30
1.2.5.6 International newspaper indexes 31
1.3 Study size 32
1.3.1 Smallshaw and Banwell Methods 33
1.3.1.1 Smallshaw identification number 33
1.3.1.2 Banwell method, index or ratio 33
1.4 Collaborative working 34
1.4.1 Working on a large study 34
1.5 Overcoming index errors 35
1.5.1 Handwriting difficulties 35

1.5.2 OCR ... 36
1.5.3 Search strategies ... 36
1.6 Organising your data ... 36
1.6.1 Systems of naming ... 37

2. Analysis ... 41
2.1 How to analyse your documentary data ... 41
2.1.1 Data completion ... 41
2.1.2 Linking data to the correct individual ... 41
2.1.3 Linking each individual to the correct family group and tree ... 42
2.1.4 Generating testable hypotheses ... 42
2.1.5 Family reconstruction ... 42
2.1.6 Study conclusions ... 42
2.2 Using maps ... 42
2.2.1 Locating ancestors using maps ... 43
2.2.2 Gazetteers ... 43
2.2.3 Sources of maps ... 43
2.2.4 Publishing old maps ... 44
2.2.5 Creating your own maps ... 45
2.2.6 Program generated maps ... 47
2.3 Statistics for distributions ... 48
2.4 Estimating lineage numbers ... 49
2.5 DNA Projects ... 51
2.5.1 Choosing a DNA testing company ... 52
2.5.2 Frequently asked DNA questions ... 53
2.5.3 Publicising your DNA project ... 54
2.5.4 Case study: The Dorling DNA project ... 55

3. Synthesis ... 58
3.1 Meaning of the surname ... 58
3.1.2 Useful websites ... 59
3.2 Origin of the surname ... 60
3.3 Lineage reconstruction ... 60
3.4 Illegitimacy rates ... 61
3.5 Evaluating progress ... 62
3.5.1 Accessibility of indexes ... 63
3.5.2 Size of the surname community ... 63
3.5.3 Size of the sample ... 63
3.5.4 Spread ... 64
3.5.5 Skill ... 64

4. Publicising your study ... 65
4.1 Magazines and Journals ... 65
4.2 Websites ... 66
4.2.1 Your own website ... 66
4.2.2 The Guild Profile ... 66
4.2.3 Registering and advertising on other websites ... 66
4.2.4 Wikipedia surname page ... 66
4.2.5 Improving your search engine rankings ... 67
4.2.5.1 Some hints on improving Google rankings ... 68
4.3 Social Networking (Facebook, etc.) ... 69
4.3.1 Facebook for one-name studies ... 69
4.3.2 Promoting your one-name study on Facebook ... 70
4.3.3 Collecting genealogy information on Facebook ... 70
4.4 New.familysearch.org ... 71

4.5 Mailshots 71
4.5.1 Garnering addresses 71
4.5.2 Who to contact 72
4.5.3 Maximising response rate 72
4.5.4 The content of the letter 72
4.5.5 Repeat mailshots 73
4.5.6 Benefits 73

5. Responding to Enquiries 74
5.1 Guild requirements 74
5.2 Etiquette 74
5.3 Managing your contacts list 75
5.3.1 Software packages 75
5.3.2 Data requirements 76
5.3.3 Paper-based solutions 76

6. Publication of results 78
6.1 One-name study articles 79
6.2 One-name study books 79
6.2.1 ONS books published by Guild members 81
6.2.2 Genealogy-related books published by Guild members 82
6.2.3 General notes on publishing a book 82
6.3 One-name study websites 82
6.3.1 Criteria for a one-name website 83
6.3.2 Creating a website 84
6.3.2.1 Web publishing software programs 85
6.4 One-name blogs 86
6.5 Privacy of living people 86
6.5.1 1998 Data Protection Act 87

7. Preserving your study 88
7.1 Safeguarding your study 88
7.1.1 Backups 88
7.1.1.1 Backup methods 89
7.2 Archiving your study 91
7.2.1 Your own archive copies 91
7.2.2 The Guild Electronic Archive 91
7.2.3 Lodging material with the Guild Library 92
7.2.4 Submitting material to the Guild Online Library 92
7.3 Bequeathing your study 93
7.4 Setting up a One-Name Society 93

Appendix: A One-Name Study Plan 95

0. Introduction to the Art of One-Name Studies

0.1 Carrying out a one-name study

> ***"The whole object of one-name research is to study the whole of a family in depth, its migrations, the relationship of the various branches, how each has developed its own line and social position, its religious and political beliefs, occupations, etc – merely collecting every instance of the name is not by any means sufficient."***
>
> – Iain Swinnerton,
> founder member and Vice President of the Guild

As Iain makes clear, the purpose of a one-name study is not the collection of data for its own sake. Its aim is to research the genealogy and family history of all persons with a given surname and its linked variants.

In doing so a study will in time find itself investigating, among other aspects:

- Early references to the name
- The name's meaning and origin
- Its links to variant and 'deviant' names
- Its frequency relative to the general population of its country of origin
- Its distribution in time and space
- The patterns of immigration and emigration associated with its development and spread.

The Guild identifies seven broad activities within a one-name study:

1) **Data collection,** comprising documentary, personal, and genetic data
2) **Analysis** of collected data
3) **Synthesis** from collected data
4) **Responding to enquiries**
5) **Publicising your study**
6) **Publication of results**
7) **Preserving your Study**

By ***Analysis*** we mean investigating the data collected to maximise the content and value of each data item and to show how they all link together.

By ***Synthesis*** we mean generating new hypotheses about the linked data in order to test the findings suggested by it. It is about drawing conclusions on the big questions relating to a surname, such as where it arose, what it means, and what are its variants.

Each of these aspects of a one-name study will be discussed in the following pages.

0.1.1 Definition of a one-name study

Surname studies started today are generally founded upon the collection of documentary event data or of DNA results, though an increasing number of studies combine the approaches, data and research methods of both.

The Guild defines a one-name study as a project researching the genealogy and family history of all persons with a given surname – or group of related surnames – as opposed to researching a particular pedigree (the ancestors of one person) or specific descendancy (the descendants of one person or couple).

To some family historians, the term "one-name studies" means something slightly different. It still means the study of people who have a common surname, but allows restrictions to be placed on the research; for example, studying only a single country or region, or a particular period in time. But Guild members with a registered name have a genuine interest in all occurrences of their study name world-wide and in all periods. Strictly speaking, what the Guild calls "one-name studies" might be better called "whole-name studies", to differentiate them from such restricted researches.

The reason the Guild is called the Guild of One-Name Studies, rather than the Guild of Whole-Name Studies, is because in its earliest days, immediately after the Guild was formed, such restricted researches were allowed, so the name was chosen accordingly. However, it soon became apparent that it would not be possible to organise a meaningful society around such studies, so the definition was altered to the one we use today – but the Guild's name was not changed to match.

The broad scope of a whole-name study enables a Guild member to investigate aspects of their research wider than those of a single-pedigree genealogist. For example, investigating changes in the geographical distribution of the surname over the centuries, or attempting to reconstruct the genealogy of as many lines as possible bearing the name. A frequent aim is to identify the original location of the name, especially if it appears to derive from a place name.

0.1.2 Hints and tips

Firstly, there is no "right" or "wrong" way to go about undertaking your study, but here are a few pointers which may help.

Organisation

- Be organised – it's easier to do when you are starting.
- Don't try to do too much at once.
- Don't get distracted.
- Create a Master Index of what documents are filed where.
- Keep a research log of what you have checked and found (or not).
- Maintain separate 'To Do' folders for each of the Archives that you intend to visit.
- Record sources in detail and save copies of web pages off-line.
- Date things (especially Family Trees).
- Identify people on photographs.

Guild resources

- Register your name and its variants.
- Create a Guild Profile Page.
- Submit your registered name to Guild Marriage Challenges, making sure you submit your information using the format described on the Marriage Challenge page of the website.
- Use the Guild Wiki, especially the many pages describing data sources for various countries.
- For recording BMD and Census returns, consider using the Guild Archive formats if you are designing your own database or spreadsheet.
- Use the Guild Forum and don't be afraid to ask questions.

- Do not feel awkward contacting one member individually rather than through the Forum.
- Get a mentor.

Your registered name

- Locate where the name originated from and focus your research on that country or county first.
- Identify variants and deviants early on.
- Use the *Surname Atlas* to help you understand the distribution of your name.

Computers

- Regularly back up your data.
- Try to keep a copy of your data elsewhere (see *7.1: Safeguarding Your Study*)
- Name your computer files logically, and keep them in folders which are also logically named.
- When using spreadsheets, keep forenames and surnames in separate columns.

Contacts

- Keep details of everyone who contacts you. If the information you currently have does not help them now, you may be able to help later.
- Try and get postal addresses – they change less frequently than email addresses. It is so frustrating to find the information that someone is looking for, only to discover their email address is no longer valid.
- Don't discount offers of help from other interested parties.
- Make use of Rootsweb's mailing list facilities.

Free resources and the internet

- Make use of UKBMD, especially for locating marriages.
- Use FreeBMD to download the UK GRO details, then use FindMyPast or Ancestry to fill in gaps.
- Use the 1880 U.S.A. Census, 1881 Canada and 1881 UK Census to locate all mentions of your chosen surname.
- Use what you find on the internet as a basis for research.
- Contact tree owners and see if they are willing to share their findings and data with you; they can only say no. But don't believe everything you find on online family trees.
- Set up a Facebook Page (see *4.3: Social Networking*).
- Rootschat has useful resources links by county.
- Investigate On-line Parish Clerks.

Other resources

Many of these can be found in Libraries and Archives Departments in the UK.

- National Burial Index
- Ancestry
- FindMyPast
- Gale Newspaper Database (Infotrac)

Finally, don't forget –

- to do the shopping, feed the family and cut the grass!

0.2 The Guild of One-Name Studies

The Guild has its roots back in 1979 promoting high-quality documentary research in the pre-computer and pre-internet era; but it positions itself today as a world-leading centre of excellence for in-depth studies of individual surnames and groups of surnames.

The Guild supports the development of one-name studies without mandating any particular approach or method, recognising that the field has been transformed in recent years by the digitisation of data, the proliferation of on-line transcriptions, and the development of genealogical DNA test applications, and aware that the field is likely to be transformed in the future by new technologies, online resources and opportunities as yet unidentified.

0.2.1 Guild membership

If you're reading this then you are probably already a member of the Guild, and you may or may not have already registered one or more study surnames.

According to the Guild's Governing Document, its Constitution, Guild membership is for anyone who has an interest in one-name studies, and defines these as "research into the genealogy and family history of all persons with the same surname and its variants".

Members of the Guild are not by any means obliged to register a study surname or to follow a one-name study themselves; it is quite acceptable just to have an interest in this field of research. However, if a Guild member does register a surname, then he or she implicitly accepts the following principles in relation to this registered name:

- that it has a global scope
- that it includes research within countries where the name is relatively significant and where sources of genealogical data are readily available
- that it researches and stores data available in core genealogical datasets and transcriptions
- that it stores and may research other data where the surname is mentioned
- that the member keeps the Study Codes up to date

In addition to this, there is one commitment that a Guild member takes on as part of registering a name: to respond, in a timely fashion, to all enquiries about that name that do not impose a financial cost in replying. This includes enquiries by email or by pre-paid letter.

Note that although the Guild specifies that a registered study must be global in scope and universal in timespan, not limited to a particular place, region, period, or family, the Guild does not require its members to follow a particular research method, or require any specific research activity, or to progress a study to any measured timetable. Nor is there any requirement to reconstruct family trees nor to supply them to enquirers. What is expected is that members will make their best efforts to assist other researchers and enquirers, even if that help is to signpost them to other researchers and resources rather than resolving their specific genealogical uncertainty. Your commitment is to reply to enquiries, it is not to actually supply the answers – although, of course, you may do so. See further in 5: Responding to Enquiries.

One-name study – documentary or genetic basis?

It has always been an assumption within the Guild that the main way to conduct a global whole-name study is through a comprehensive programme of documentary research. In the past, for example when the Guild was formed in 1979, this was the only way to carry out a whole-name study. However, technology changes mean that this is no longer the case. It is still assumed that members will at some point embark on a comprehensive programme of documentary research, but it is not a requirement to do so at the start of a registered surname study. For example, some whole-name studies now begin with a focus on collecting genetic data; all studies have to start somewhere, and an interest in DNA testing is as good a place as any. However, to continue with only DNA testing would be to place a restriction on the study and so not meet the requirements of registration. It is therefore anticipated that such a study would in due course develop a detailed documentary research programme of the traditional kind. But no timeframe is laid down for this to begin.

0.2.2 How the Guild can help your one-name study

0.2.2.1 Guild services and facilities

The Guild is extremely active in a number of areas, and all members, new and long standing, are encouraged to participate and use all our facilities as they wish.

Reading materials

- The *Journal of One-Name Studies*, posted quarterly to members with news, articles and ideas on this branch of family history. All issues are available online as PDFs and can be accessed via the *Journal* page on the website. The last four issues (i.e. the last year's *Journals*) are available only to members; earlier issues are available to the general public. There is also a JournalSearch facility on the *Journal* page of the website allowing you to find articles by subject or by author or by publication date.
- The *Members Handbook* (last updated in September 2011), which details how best to undertake a one-name study. A copy can be downloaded as a 37-page PDF file from the Members Room.
- There are dozens of high quality entries in the Guild's 2009 Publication Award Competition and the 2010 and 2011 Essay Competitions, many of which can be viewed on the website or borrowed using the Online Library Catalogue also on the website.
- The Guild has a collection of articles about documentary research, Guild facilities, and DNA projects, which are available from the Members Room of the website.
- Also in the Members Room are a selection of presentations prepared by Guild members and officers which explain aspects of one-name studies and the Guild's activities.
- Finally the Members Room has a list of URLs of useful websites as submitted by Guild members.

Direct research assistance

There are a number of facilities available in the Members Room of the Guild website which can assist in members' research:

- The Guild Marriage Index, a service to help members find the names of marriage partners and identify the locations of post-1837 marriages in England and Wales
- Guild Marriage Challenges, both ongoing and completed, where members volunteer to search for marriage entries submitted for registered surnames in the Parish Registers of a Registration District (England and Wales) for the period 1837-1911

- The Guild Probate Index, which allows members to search for surnames mentioned in Wills which are different from that of the testator
- The Guild Scottish Index, which indexes all surnames referenced in Scottish marriage entries (not just the bride and groom)
- The Random Acts of Genealogical Kindness project (RAOGK), where members offer or request specific lookup services
- Look-ups in various significant databases
- Promotional discounts on genealogical services for members.

Meeting and talking

- The Guild's online discussion Forum hosted on Rootsweb allows subscribers to tap into the deep expertise of our members on a wide range of topics.
- Regular seminars are held in various parts of Britain, and increasingly overseas too, on different aspects of one-name studies. Where possible, proceedings of past seminars are posted on to the Members Room of the website for the benefit of members who cannot attend the seminars in person.
- Meetings organised by Regional Reps bring members together to share expertise. Planned meetings are listed in the Regional Reps area of the Members Room.
- The Guild partners with Pharos, who run online courses on a wide range of genealogical subjects including two courses specifically on One-Name Studies.
- The Guild runs an Annual Conference in April each year.

Project support

- Members can set up a Profile page, based on a simple template, for their one-name study within the Guild website. Members report that this is a very effective way to attract enquirers via internet search engines.
- Email aliases within the one-name.org domain are available to all members, in the form your.name@one-name.org and yourregisteredsurname@one-name.org. Emails to these aliases are redirected to your personal email address, so that if you change your email address you need only ask the Guild to re-point the alias. There is more advice on this below, in *0.3.3.1: Using your Guild email alias*.
- The Guild offers an email DNA advisory service, giving advice to members about all aspects of genetic testing within the context of a surname study, including help to set up your own Y-chromosome surname project. This is accessed by emailing the special Guild DNA Helpline at DNA@one-name.org.
- Data that members have transcribed for their study surname can be published on the Guild website using the Guild's Electronic Archive.
- Since Guild members are mostly extensive users of computers, the Guild offers an email computer alert service (WARP; or Warning, Advice and Reporting Point) to provide expert and timely advice on computer threats.
- Contact details of any member can be found using the Guild's Register of One-Name Studies.
- The Chairman produces an occasional email Newsflash of late-breaking news to members who have opted to receive it.
- A list of Skype users is maintained on the Guild website to encourage communications among members.

Support the Guild

- The Guild Committee and Subcommittee meeting Agenda and Minutes are published in the Members Room.
- The Guild is run entirely by unpaid volunteers and an estimated 5-8% of members do at least one thing a year to support the Guild. When you're ready to get involved, offer your services by emailing the Guild's Chairman at chairman@one-name.org or the Volunteers Coordinator at volunteers@one-name.org.
- Members also contribute the specialist knowledge they hold to the Wiki (and hence to this book which was created from the Wiki).

0.3 Using a computer for one-name studies

Do backups! And if possible keep a copy away from home!

0.3.1 Computer requirements

A one-namer's computer will be asked to perform a range of inter-related tasks:

- storing data – in a spreadsheet or database
- processing data to identify linkages
- retaining and displaying data in a format that can conveniently be shared with other researchers – such as the GEDCOM format
- communicating with other researchers – via an email program or webmail account
- publishing the study's results – on a website, as a PDF, or as a book.

0.3.2 Choice of operating system

Genealogy programs are available for the Windows, Mac and Linux platforms, though the greatest choice is on Windows.

New Windows PC systems being sold today are generally 64-bit machines. However, many Windows programs used by genealogists have not been upgraded from 32-bit to 64-bit compatibility; many never will be. Additionally, some that work on Windows-XP may not work in Windows-7. Members report that using the Windows-7 Ultimate edition allows you to create a separate space on the PC to run previous versions such as Windows-XP in which older programs should function as on older machines. Mac users report that they can partition their hard drive to allow different operating systems, such as Windows, to run in parallel simultaneously with the Mac OS.

In the past few years a new type of portable PC has become available: the netbook. These are lighter than laptops, have smaller screens (usually 10"), and generally carry fewer features and peripherals. Most have a much greater battery life than laptops. Almost all will connect with the web via a Wifi link and use a USB port to share data via a thumb drive rather than a DVD or CD drive. Netbooks can be very useful as tools to take on research trips to places like Record Offices. At home, an external screen can be plugged in for easier viewing especially for looking at large spreadsheets.

Members will certainly need a full suite of programs and online services to protect their work. These would include a broadband internet connection – preferably a fast one, external back up (to a second hard drive) and to an online backup service (such as Mozy, Carbonite, and others). It's also an idea to share your data with one or more trusted researchers on an annual basis. A specialist back-up program, such as Acronis, can be set up to make a full disk back-up supplemented by incremental back-ups on a daily basis. Backups are dealt with more fully in *7.1: Safeguarding your study* below.

0.3.3 Choice of email systems

Members have the option to download messages from their standard POP email account using a traditional piece of desktop software such as Microsoft Outlook, or to use one of the many online services such as Gmail or Hotmail. The online services offer several distinct advantages: they are very efficient at filtering out spam mail automatically, access to them can be shared among researchers, and they offer simple but efficient ways to search and file messages. One option is to use an online account and set its preferences to forward all email sent to your @one-name.org address(es) to your standard POP account. That way you get the best of both worlds. Both types of system allow you to set up mailing lists to email files to fellow researchers and suchlike.

Another tip is to set up a separate online account that you use purely to post messages on the web or to log in to family history websites. You can always drop this address if spam traffic becomes too intense, though Gmail is highly efficient in removing it in any case.

0.3.3.1 Using your Guild email alias

In addition to the detailed notes in the Members' Handbook and the Guild website, members have noted the following tips on redirecting different Guild addresses to separate email accounts.

Redirecting different Guild addresses to separate email accounts

The Guild offers members the opportunity to adopt two email alias addresses. One is your registered surname and the second is your personal name. (Of course, if you have more than one registered name, you will have more than one study email alias.)

Some members might find it useful to use these two addresses in different ways. For example, to use the registered name address to communicate with researchers involved in the study, while reserving the personal address for another purpose such as one's own research. One reason for making this split is that, should you wish to pass on your study to someone else, they can inherit the registered surname address whilst you keep your personal one.

At present, the Guild does not offer facilities to re-direct email traffic to different 'real' email addresses. However, there are workarounds to achieve the same end. If you use an email program such as Outlook you can set up a "rule" to have the alias emails automatically forwarded to other email addresses. Alternatively, if you use a standard ISP and download incoming emails to your PC, you can set up a Gmail account and use the filters in Gmail to redirect email traffic from each Guild address to different ISPs or accounts. If you already access your email traffic in 'the cloud' with accounts at Gmail, Hotmail and the like, you can similarly set up an automatic filter to re-deliver incoming email traffic to two different accounts.

0.3.4 Choice of internet browser

In addition to Microsoft's Internet Explorer, open-source Windows browsers such as Firefox (Mozilla), Opera, Safari, and Google Chrome are viable alternatives and may offer selective advantages. From time to time, some members report that one browser or another may have problems working with parts of some websites, including commercial family history sites.

There is, however, no need to choose between the browsers available. You can download all of them and use whichever you prefer, or whichever is more appropriate to the task at hand. You can even use more than one of them at the same time. They are, after all, just programs.

Bookmarks

The Favourites/Bookmark facility in the browser keeps a list of sites you wish to revisit or remember. Another option is to record these sites in a service like Delicious (http://delicious.com) which will download a copy to your browser's own bookmark file each time you log off.

0.3.5 Choice of family-tree software

Family tree software is computer software used to record, organise, and publish genealogical data such as that collected as a one-name study and link the individuals together into family trees. Family tree software allows the user to collect data on the date and place of an individual's birth, baptism, marriage, death and burial. Most programs allow the user to include additional data on events in the individual's life such as censuses and wills. The more advanced programs will allow the inclusion of photographs, multimedia and source citations. Reports and charts can be generated from the data.

Most genealogy software allows the export of data in GEDCOM format, which can then be shared with people using different genealogy software. Some genealogy applications, such as Family Historian, use GEDCOM internally and therefore work directly with GEDCOM data.

A number of programs are available offering a variety of features. Most programs have free downloadable demos available from their websites.

The following comparison charts provide information on the features available in the various programs:

- Wikipedia's comparison of genealogy software at http://en.wikipedia.org/wiki/Comparison_of_genealogy_software

- Genealogy software review from Top Ten Reviews, at http://www.genealogy-software-review.toptenreviews.com

- My History website's comparison of some popular programs, see http://www.my-history.co.uk/acatalog/softwarecomparisonMH/compare_15.html

The Genealogy Software Review website provides user reviews of all the major family tree programs, at http://www.gensoftreviews.com/index.php.

The choice of genealogy software is very much a personal preference, but when choosing a program for a one-name study the following features are useful:

- ability to store data for unrelated individuals
- ability to record quarter dates for births, marriages and deaths from the General Register Office indexes for England and Wales
- ability to record detailed source citations
- ability to compare and merge data from two different GEDCOM files
- ability to generate reports for selected branches and family lines to send out in response to enquiries

Facebook poll

In June 2011 a poll on family-tree software was taken on the Guild's Facebook page. People were asked to answer the question "Which family history software program do you use?" A total of 226 votes were cast. Users were able to vote for more than one program, so the numbers do not add up to 226. The family tree programs, ranked in order of votes, are as given in the table:

Program	*Users*
Family Tree Maker	58
Family Historian	23
The Master Genealogist	16
Roots Magic	14
Legacy	12
Brothers Keeper	7
Personal Ancestral File	8
Reunion	6
Pedigree / Peditree	4
Filemaker	3
Ancestral Quest	1
Generations	1
Geves	1
Ifamily	1
Masterfile MPRO	1

Votes were also cast for the following computer programs which can be useful for a one-name study but are not dedicated family-tree-building programs:

Program	*Users*
Excel	39
Custodian	16
Access	5
TNG (The Next Generation)	4
Second Site	2
Libre Office	1
Lotus Approach	1
MySQL	1

0.3.6 Spreadsheets for One-Name Studies

As the table above shows, Excel (a spreadsheet program) is very popular for maintaining one-name study data.

Spreadsheets can be a useful way of storing some of your one-name study data, and particularly for indexed material such as birth, marriage and death records and census indexes. The most popular spreadsheet program is Excel, which is included in Microsoft Office packages. Other spreadsheet programs are freely available such as Open Office. Free online spreadsheet programs such as Google Docs or Windows Live SkyDrive can also be used.

Guild member John Coldwell has written a very useful two-part article in *JOONS* on computing for beginners which contains advice on the use of spreadsheets. The relevant issues of *JOONS* can be downloaded from the Guild website:

- *Computing for beginners. Part 1. Computers and the Web. JOONS* April 2009, Vol.10, No.2, pp 6-9.
- *Computing For ONS Beginners. Part 2. Spreadsheets. JOONS* July 2009, Vol.10, No.3, pp 17-19.

The latter article contains a link to a spreadsheet template which provides advice on downloading births, marriages and deaths in England and Wales from the General Register Office indexes on the FreeBMD website.

There is also some useful material about Excel from various Guild Seminars, much of which has now been made available online on the Guild website. This includes presentations and spreadsheet templates from the Computing Seminar which was held in Epsom in August 2010, which can be accessed from the Seminars area in the Members Room; this also gives access to the material from the Data Capture seminar held in Durham in August 2008.

0.3.6.1 Spreadsheets for birth, marriage and death (BMD) indexes

Many Guild members use spreadsheets to store birth, marriage and death indexes. For surnames originating in England and Wales it is now an easy matter to extract all the relevant index entries for your study name from the FreeBMD website. Coverage is now almost complete, at least up until 1930. The gaps and the later years can be filled in from one of the online subscription services such as Ancestry or Findmypast.

In order to make the best of use Guild services it is a good plan to organise your spreadsheet from the outset in a format which is compatible with the Guild's Marriage Challenges, Guild Marriage Index and Guild Electronic Archive. The Marriage Challenges and Marriage Index focus primarily on marriages in England and Wales from the period 1837 to 1911, though marriages in Australia, Scotland and America have also been included in some Marriage Challenges. The Guild Electronic Archive was initially designed for the upload of spreadsheets for births, marriages and deaths from the England and Wales BMD indexes from 1837 through to the present, but the service has now been expanded to accommodate a wider range of data from other sources including user-defined input.

The format of the spreadsheets used for these three services is not completely consistent but so long as the data is arranged in the appropriate columns it is an easy matter to copy and paste columns into the required position. In particular, for English and Welsh marriages it is advisable to use separate columns for the volumes and page numbers. If you expand your spreadsheets to include additional data such as the precise date of marriage, it helps to use separate columns for the day, month and year of marriage to make the spreadsheet compatible with the format used in the Marriage Index and the Marriage Challenges. Similarly, if you record the spouse name for marriages in your spreadsheets, it helps to use separate columns for the spouse forename and surname.

A template for the Marriage Challenges is provided in the Members Room and can be downloaded from there. This template is in a format compatible with that used for producing Marriage-Challenge "faux certificates", using the enhanced version of Andrew Millard's faux-certificate production facility, as announced in the *Journal,* October 2009, Vol10 No.4.

Samples of spreadsheets used by Guild members to record BMDs can be found in the Guild Wiki under the page title *Spreadsheets for one-name studies.*

Guild members who need help with spreadsheets can contact the Guild mentoring service at mentors@one-name.org to ask for assistance. The mentee will be matched with a suitable mentor.

0.4 The art of searching

This is a key skill which a one-name study researcher needs to develop.
Remember when searching that the site index will probably include transcription and other errors. A degree of lateral thinking and patience is often required when inserting the search details before that elusive data can be found. Wild card searching can be helpful especially for finding variant names.

Search using different sites with the same data, as the search options and transcription errors may differ. Switching between sites can also help. For example it may be possible to locate a marriage and place in FreeBMD helping to locate a census entry giving age and place of birth.

Web sites appear to be designed primarily to meet the needs of the "own family history" researchers requiring only a few names. One-name study (except rare name studies) researchers on the other hand often need many hundreds if not thousands of names where access to each individual image would be prohibitively time consuming. Once again one-name study researchers have to use lateral thinking to maximise the data that can be extracted from the free-to-access index.

Experiment with different search tactics to elicit extra information. For example when searching the England and Wales birth registrations for 1916-2005, try inserting the study name as the mother's maiden name in the search. From the children's names you can see the father's surname and where the child's name is the study name it may indicate that a father's name was not provided.

0.4.1 Useful programs

When downloading census images, it helps to use the reference number, e.g. RG9_0405_f126_p30.gif as the file name. But of course you will collect a very large number of images with names of this form.

The free shell extension ***Shell Tools*** from Moon Software contains a utility called ***Filenote*** which creates a text file with the same name as the image – or indeed any – file that you right-click on. Use this utility to store details of the image and any notes relating to it. You can find this at http://www.moonsoftware.com/shelltools.asp.

Icon positions depend on screen resolution but can be remembered separately for each screen using the simple program ***Desktop_Resetter*** (http://www.desktility.com).

Operating systems provide a wide range of keyboard short cuts, and it is well worth learning a few of these. Perhaps the most used are Ctrl and c together (**Ctrl+c**) to copy highlighted data and Ctrl and v together (**Ctrl+v**) to paste the data into another place.

One key which is often overlooked, perhaps because it is very badly named, is the **Print Screen** key, which takes a snapshot of the screen for pasting into a word processor document (using Ctrl+v). **Alt + Print Screen** takes a snapshot of the webpage you are viewing, rather than of the whole screen (i.e. it misses off all the surrounding stuff about your own system).

Personal keyboard shortcuts can be created using the free ***auto-hotkey*** program from http://www.autohotkey.com. It includes a comprehensive manual and is relatively easy to use. For example the following three-line "script" is used to set up a shortcut key to automatically type your email address into a document or website:

```
#e::
Send, goons.member@one_name.com
Return
```

In the above you would of course include your email address in place of the made-up address used in the example. The line "#e::" determines which shortcut keys to use – in this case the "windows key" (which is denoted by #) with the "e" key. Many other keys can be used and the program allows a choice to be made. The program can include many scripts for other uses including for example, inserting your study name or your postal address, and can save a lot of typing.

Firefox provides useful free "add-ons" that improve the capabilities of the basic browser. The ***Table2Clipboard*** add-on is particularly helpful for an ONS, as it allows a complete large table of data on a web site to be quickly copied. To do this, right-click the mouse anywhere on the table and then select "Copy whole table" from the displayed menu. The table is copied to the clipboard, from which it can easily be pasted into another application such as Excel or Open Office Calc.

File renamer basic (http://tinyurl.com/yzxkwne) is a very useful program if you suddenly decide to change your naming system for all your data files. You can rename files, folders, and MP3 files. It has a filename filter so you can easily narrow down your search to a specific type of file or filename to work with. You can also remove x number of characters starting from x-character, and find and replace text.

Karen's Directory Printer (http://www.karenware.com/powertools/ptdirprn.asp) will let you print the name of every file on a drive, along with the file's size, date and time of last modification, and attributes (Read-Only, Hidden, System and Archive).

Puretext or ***Puretext Plus*** is a free-to-use program that will copy text from web pages and strip off all the html formatting. See http://stevemiller.net/puretext or http://code.google.com/p/puretext-plus.

1. Data collection

Data collection is the first and most enduring activity of any one-name study, and documentary data will be the principal aspect of it.

Whereas most family history research tends to ***converge*** as it focuses on finding specific ancestors and collateral connections, by contrast the research within a one-name study tends to ***diverge***, widening as each new reference potentially opens up a new area of enquiry. With traditional ancestor hunting, the search goes cold if you can't prove the next generation back. A one-name study, however, takes an interest in the continuous presence of a name irrespective of whether the references we are able to collect can be assembled into family groups.

To capture the scope of a one-name study you need to explore as much indexed data as possible. Indexes, together with "calendars", resumés and some directories are known as meta-data, i.e. created data pointing to original data. Traditional family history emphasises that one should always check the original primary data, and not rely on the secondary indexes alone. Ideally, one-namers should do the same, though the large scale of many studies limits this.

Guild studies are world-wide endeavours and collecting worldwide data is a never-ending task. Members will find that they will prioritise their proactive data collection efforts, most likely to within the country of origin, while continuing passively retaining data that they come across or is submitted by others. In fact, seasoned one-namers will admit ruefully that almost any kind of genealogical source is relevant to a one-name study, as are many sources containing surname data which are not normally recognised as genealogical.

As a check-list, consider the following classes of data, initially concentrating on indexed sources:

- Vital Records: births, marriages and deaths of course, but also baptisms, burials, adoptions and divorces; post mortem inquests; monumental inscriptions; bastardy examinations; wills and administrations.

- Place data: censuses, street directories, telephone directories, Electoral Rolls, property deeds, militia lists, tithe records, glebe terriers, manorial records.
- Educational data: school records, university alumni, degree lists.
- Occupational data: censuses again, apprentice records, manorial records, military service records, trades directories (many of which are online), professional directories, Livery Companies, Manorial records.
- Mobility data: settlement certificates, immigration (e.g. Castle Garden and Ellis Island), emigration, ships' passenger lists, aliens registration and naturalisation records.
- Taxation records: Lay subsidies, Poll Tax, Hearth Tax, Window Tax, Land Tax, death duties.
- Other life events: criminal and court records, Poor Law records, workhouse records, official Gazettes, newspapers, religious records, patent records.
- Emails from enquirers can provide valuable insight into the genealogy and family history of a family, as well as providing data not available from public sources. They should, though, always be taken with a pinch of salt.
- Heraldic records: Official (College of Arms), unofficial (Burke's General Armory), Heralds' visitations
- Assembled biographies, pedigrees and histories
- Photographs
- Maps

Having collected the data, there are a number of ways in which it can be organised and stored – see *1.6: Organising your data* below.

Whilst a one-name study can be carried out by one person, it is often more effective if more are involved. This can be especially true with data collection and, if the benefits are to be fully realised, it may be useful to collaborate with other researchers; see below, *1.4: Collaborative Working*.

1.1 Starting to collect data

1.1.1 Collecting documentary data

Registering a study surname with the Guild means that you should regard your one-name study as being global in scope, and that you will "research within countries where the name is relatively significant and where sources of genealogical data are readily available." While members are expected to strive towards collecting a substantial body of documentary data from "core genealogical datasets and transcriptions", the Guild deliberately provides no definition of what such core datasets should consist of, as this is certain to differ markedly from one country to another.

But the Guild does offer a recommendation that, for countries of the world where the name is relatively significant and where resources are readily accessible, members should plan to collect (potentially over an extended period of time) available data from:

- national indexes of births, marriages and deaths.
- indexes to national censuses.
- major will indexes.
- large-scale transcription projects such as the International Genealogical Index.
- key websites with transcribed data such as FamilySearch (www.familysearch.org).

The Guild Wiki contains many pages ("Sources for … ") detailing the available documentary records in various countries, with in many cases links to online search facilities. These are not reproduced here since the Wiki provides an ideal gateway to these data websites and is easily and frequently updated. In addition, the Guild website contains in the Members Room a list of useful URLs.

Two items of general advice when starting out:

1) Collect the largest datasets first: this would be the first two sources shown above.
2) Always think about the veracity of the data you're using. Trust transcribed data more than anecdotal information, and primary data before secondary data.

1.1.2 Collecting genetic data

The earliest Y-chromosome DNA surname projects have already been underway for more than a decade, and with more than 5,000 registered projects containing an estimated 15,000 surnames they are now well established as a mainstream genealogical activity. That said, you cannot reconstruct a family tree without the documentary data to back it up, and many Guild members feel that their present priority is to focus on the documentary aspect of their study.

A growing number of Guild members are at the forefront of applying DNA testing to their surname studies, and there is plenty of useful information about this both on the Guild website and later in this book. It should be noted, though, that running a successful DNA test programme may demand a great deal of time and energy from its organiser. Guild members should note that it is common practice to outsource the administration of the DNA project to another researcher outside of the Guild, and such arrangements generally work very well.

1.1.3 Collecting data from living name-bearers

Documentary records are often not available to cover the most recent period of our history, and the best means to bridge that gap is by collecting data from name-bearers either first-hand or from other researchers. Either way, this can best be done through an active programme of contact-making and discussion, seeking out family members to ask them for details of their immediate family. Online bulletin boards are often a good way to meet other name-bearers, though traditional means such as mailshots and phone calls can still prove useful as well as online social networks such as Facebook. Many more details are given below under *4: Publicising your study*.

1.1.4 Data collection summary

It is good practice that at a relatively early stage of its development a one-name study organiser identifies and surveys the available documentary sources likely to be of most use to their study, assesses the potential benefits of a parallel Y-chromosome DNA project, and works out a strategy to collect data from living name-bearers and researchers.

1.2 Sources of documentary data

The Guild website Wiki gives many resources for data collection in specific countries. But there are many resources for surname-related data which span several countries or are even global in extent. Some of the most important of these are listed below.

1.2.1 Vital data from the LDS (IGI, VRI, FamilySearch)

The best-known resource covering vital data in multiple countries is the International Genealogical Index (IGI) augmented by the Vital Records Indexes. These are provided by the Genealogical Society of Utah (GSU), which is the genealogical arm of the Church of Jesus Christ of Latter-day Saints (LDS, commonly referred to as the Mormons). The LDS uses the name FamilySearch for many of its public-facing activities, and as part of its mission collects, and provides free access to, genealogical data worldwide.

1.2.1.1 International Genealogical Index

The International Genealogical Index or IGI is a worldwide index created by the LDS. It contains mainly baptisms and marriages, and varies in its coverage from place to place.

It also varies in its reliability. Where the LDS has transcribed data from parish registers (denoted by "*Extracted marriage record for locality listed in the record*" in the Message section of the output display), this is generally more reliable than that supplied by individuals ("*Patron Submissions*"). Patron submissions should be treated with caution and all data checked with original sources. To understand more about the nature of the data collected here it is worth reading an account in the Berkshire FHS journal: http://www.berksfhs.org.uk/journal/Jun2001/jun2001SomeIGIConfusionsUntangled.htm, and a more detailed account from a Mormon perspective by Helen Schatvet Ullmann: http://www.livgenmi.com/fhcigi.htm.

Note that the IGI is an index, not a transcription. Consequently, the original might contain more information than is given in its IGI entry. So, even for extracted entries, it can be worth while checking the original.

The IGI is available at many LDS Family History Centres and other libraries. Much of the IGI can be found on-line at http://www.familysearch.org, though the coverage is not the same as you will find at LDS Family History Centres.

One-namers can search baptisms and marriages for their name by parish within town within county within country, using independently produced batch-number indexes. For Britain, there is the facility developed by Hugh Wallis at

http://freepages.genealogy.rootsweb.com/~hughwallis/IGIBatchNumbers.htm

while for Germany there is

http://www.igi-index.de/

owned by Christoph Wahler.

Record extractions created since about 1990 by the LDS are no longer being added to the IGI but to the LDS Vital Records Indexes (see next section).

1.2.1.2 Vital Records Indexes

The Vital Records Indexes (VRI) are data transcriptions from parish registers. Any new transcriptions by the LDS will be put in the VRIs, rather than the International Genealogical Index which will now be used only for patron submissions.

Only the VRIs for Scandinavia and Mexico are available at the FamilySearch website http://www.familysearch.org. However, VRIs for the British Isles (second edition), Australia, and North America are available on CD-ROM. There is a useful summary of numbers of baptisms and marriages covered by county and parish with FHL film numbers and years covered on the Genoot website at http://www.genoot.com/downloads/BVRI2/.

1.2.1.3 Obtaining copies of documents through the LDS

You can order a wide range of records if they have been filmed by the LDS. The familysearch.org website has a link to the Family History Library Catalogue, which will list all the films available. The cost has recently increased to $7.50 (USA and Canada) for a loan of up to 90 days for each roll of microfilm ($4.75 for microfiche).

The request form is available at http://www.familysearch.org/films/. You will need to have registered for an account with FamilySearch in order to request loans of films. Your requested films will be made available to you at your designated local Family History Centre.

1.2.2 UK Vital Data Sources

1.2.2.1 England and Wales – the GRO

The General Register Office indexes provide a major source for vital data for one-name studies in England and Wales. In theory, all birth, marriage and death registrations from July 1837 are indexed. Since the closure of the Family Record Centre in London, the original indexes are no longer available in book format. However they are available as microfilm or microfiche copies at libraries, record offices and LDS Family History Centres throughout the world.

Copies of the index are now also to be found on the Internet. The FreeBMD project has substantially completed transcribing the birth, marriage and death index entries from 1837 to the 1930s into a searchable database format at http://www.freebmd.org.uk. Also, FreeBMD has posted a complete set of page images for the period 1837 to 1983 on the Ancestry website (http://www.ancestry.com/search/rectype/vital/freebmd/bmd.aspx). Both the images and the partial database are free.

Pay-per-view sites such as FindMyPast (http://www.findmypast.co.uk) may be easier to search, especially when the original index is erroneous. FindMyPast also has the "Miscellaneous Indexes" and FamilyRelatives (http://www.familyrelatives.com/index.php) has a fully transcribed database for 1866-1920. In addition, FamilyRelatives offer free access to the GRO Overseas records, and have a detailed list of them at http://www.familyrelatives.com/information/info_detail.php?id=34.

The indexes for the period 1984 to 2004 are produced in database format by the GRO, and can be consulted on Ancestry (by subscribers only) and on the pay-to-view sites mentioned above, as well as on BMDindex (http://www.thegenealogist.co.uk/nameindex/). Here searches can be made for free which return much of the information – you need only pay to view the actual reference numbers, plus the mother's maiden name in the birth index and date of birth in the death index. However it does allow reverse lookups on the spouse surname for the marriages.

The indexes from 2005 onwards are available as microfiche only at these centres:

- Birmingham Central Library
- Bridgend Reference and Information Library
- The British Library
- City of Westminster Archives Centre
- Greater Manchester County Record Office
- Plymouth Central Library

The Guild has established a project for members to request look-ups of their registered names in the post-2005 indexes by emailing GRO-BMD-2005@one-name.org.

The indexes alone can be very useful in compiling data about a name, even without the purchase of certificates. The information they show has altered over time, as follows:-

- **Birth Index:** 1911 September quarter: mother's maiden name starts to be shown.
- **Marriage Index:** 1912 March quarter: spouse's former name starts to be shown.
- **Death Index:** 1866 March quarter: age at death starts to be shown.
- **Death Index:** 1969, June quarter: age at death replaced by date of birth.
- **Adoption Index**: 1947: Year of birth starts to be given
- **All BMD indexes:** 1984 on: registrations shown by month, rather than by quarter

Multiple spouse surnames

Generally the GRO indexers were as comprehensive as possible, indexing all possible surnames of the bride and groom and their fathers. Consequently, sometimes one sees an entry of the form:

Haywood Frederick G.......Jackson or Brayshaw.......Lancaster 10c 1552

The multiple surnames for the spouse may have a number of causes:

- If the father's surname differs from the person being married, both will be indexed. This may be due to adoption, fostering, a step-father's name being given or one of the reasons below;
- If a woman was widowed or divorced, and declared her former married surname, then that will be indexed as well as her father's surname;
- If the couple have been living together using one of their surnames and one of them declares that he or she is 'known as' a surname, that will be indexed as well as their other surname(s).

Acquiring birth, marriage or death certificates

Once the index entry has been found for the event, a formal certificate of birth, marriage or death can be ordered online from the GRO. The cost will be £9.25 per certificate.

Marriage Challenges

Because the information available from the GRO indexes is limited, and because the full marriage certificate is so expensive (prohibitive for most one-name studies), the Guild has instituted a "Marriage Challenge" project. This is a mutual support project, where one Guild member (the 'Challenger') volunteers to find the details of marriages for other members (the 'Requesters'). The simplicity of the idea has led to it becoming probably the most popular project ever launched by the Guild.

A marriage is, of course, a key event in family history and can often reveal important family details, much more than the indexes. The vast majority of marriages took place in an Anglican church, and most of the marriage registers from those churches are deposited in a County Record Office. So the principle of a Marriage Challenge is that a Guild member local to a County Record Office will choose an appropriate Registration District covered by that CRO, and offer to look up marriages for other members with study names marrying in that Registration District who can provide the GRO index details.

1.2.2.2 Scotland – GROS

The General Register Office for Scotland (GROS) has a rather more obliging attitude to making its records accessible online, and the website ScotlandsPeople (http://www.scotlandspeople.gov.uk) is the official Scottish genealogy resource. It is a pay-per-view site, where the user pays for pages of index entries and for certificate images, but the site provides a free surname search to show what data exists. It is worth observing that instead of paying £9.25 for a paper certified copy of a register entry as with the GRO, the ScotlandsPeople website can provide an electronic "office copy" of a register page (normally in TIFF format) for little more than £1.00.

Note also that Scottish birth, marriage and death register entries are usually much more informative than their English equivalents, and since in Scotland married women do not lose their maiden names there can be much more surname data available than in England and Wales. However, central registration did not start in Scotland until 1855, as against 1837 for England and Wales.

1.2.2.3 Northern Ireland – GRONI

The General Register Office for Northern Ireland (GRONI) has a website for genealogists and family historians, with the URL: http://www.nidirect.gov.uk/index/information-and-services/leisure-home-and-community/history-heritage-and-museums/archive-for-family-and-local-history.htm.

It offers an online search facility for the 1901 and 1911 census of Ireland, but as yet does not provide any online search facilities for birth, marriage or death registrations or indexes. There is a computerised index but it can only be searched in person in the GRONI public search room (booking a place is advisable).

Central registration of births, deaths and marriages in Northern Ireland started in 1864.

1.2.3 Vital data for other countries

Countries differ in the data accessible for research. A good and increasing level of detail on sources for many countries is maintained in the Guild Wiki.

1.2.4 Other sources of vital data

Deaths of people from many nations can be found at:

- Commonwealth War Graves Commission (http://www.cwgc.org)
- Find a Grave (http://www.findagrave.com)
- Interment.net (Cemetery Transcription Library) (http://www.interment.net)

Other useful links and resources include:

- The WorldGenWeb Project (http://worldgenweb.org)
- Genealogy and Family History Internet Web Directory (http://www.academic-genealogy.com/index.htm)
- Roots Web mailing lists (http://lists.rootsweb.com)

1.2.5 Biographical and residential data

Useful biographical and residential data, but mostly without any indication of birth or death dates, can be harvested for several nations at once via the following resources, described more fully below:

- Web Search Engines
- Book Indexes
- Indexes of Patents
- Reports of Case Law
- Biographical Indexes
- International Newspaper Indexes
- Phone Book of the World

1.2.5.1 Web search engines

Web search engines store information about a large number of web pages. A program known as a web crawler collects the complete text of web pages by following every link it sees. Data about the web pages is then stored in an index database for use in later queries.

These indexes contain, among other things, millions of surnames which will be of interest to the one-name researcher.

Typical finds include:

- personal web pages of persons using your study name
- staff lists and business awards
- alumni lists of schools and colleges, and accounts of sports teams
- local history pages and freelance transcriptions of vital records indexes
- magazine and newspaper articles

It is important to understand that the engines only search readable web pages. Most private and corporate databases that can be accessed via the internet, for example the http://www.familysearch.org site, must be searched individually and their content will not be spotted by a regular web search.

For many surname researchers, a major difficulty with web searching is that surnames may also be in use as first names or as ordinary words in one of the world's languages. For example, it is extremely difficult to track persons surnamed *Merry* or *Christmas* because there are so many Noel greetings on the web.

The best strategy to overcome this problem is to develop a list of exclusions. In a Google search, for example, this is constructed by preceding the exclusion word with a minus sign, for example: "Christmas -merry -happy -"new year" -greetings -season -shopping".

A very effective way to highlight academic articles and books written by persons with surnames of interest is via **Google Scholar** (http://scholar.google.co.uk). Similarly **Google Books** (http://www.books.google.com). Both can be searched for the surname of interest.

A useful feature with **Google** is the personalised search, which keeps a record of which sites you find interesting and which ones you exclude. This helps to improve the rankings in your personal research and avoid repeating vain searches. Also useful is the **Giga Alert** (http://www.googlealert.com) (formerly Google Alert) service, which can be activated after an initial search to detect newly arrived websites on the internet that mention your name. Despite appearances, Giga Alert is not affiliated to the Google company. A similar service is provided by Google as **Google Alerts** at http://www.google.com/alerts.

While general search engines treat a surname as if it was any other word, semantic search engines such as **ZoomInfo** (http://www.zoominfo.com/Search) specifically index personal names. Although it has a focus on "business professionals" (33 million at last count), many people are listed in connection with academic work or hobbies.

While the search results sometimes seem unwittingly daft to a human mind, ZoomInfo is an extraordinarily capable robot and a very useful tool if your study name is easily confused with another common word such as hedges, grey, carpenter, etc. or a placename. Like Google, it often offers cached copies of pages which may no longer be available in the original.

A new search engine, **Mocavo** (http://www.mocavo.com/) aimed specifically at genealogical searches, was launched in 2011. Unlike other search engines, Mocavo limits its searches solely to genealogy sites – about a million sites currently. Although it initially concentrated on American websites, it is expanding to a more global reach. Mocavo searches are not limited to names, but can include towns, states, occupations, relatives or any other text information which may be included with an ancestor's name. The "simple search" is available free of charge, but requires registration. Advanced search options including wild card searches and proximity searches (find two words that are NEAR each other, but not necessarily adjacent) are only available in a subscription version, **Mocavo Plus**.

There are some other semantic search-engines that hunt for names, such as **Wink** (http://wink.com/) or **isearch** (http://www.isearch.com), but these are mainly focussed on "social networks" with an emphasis on bloggers and chatters. They can come up with a surprising number of name matches.

Because web pages often disappear from the internet after just a few months, it is essential to create your own private cache of any pages that are of especial interest. A browser can do so easily with its **File** menu, **Save as...** command. It is usually best to save the entire page and not just its text elements. You are not allowed to re-publish these pages, but keeping copies on your own computer is acceptable as fair dealing.

It is also prudent to track the websites you find with a database. Suitable fields include:

- the URL
- the date when you saw the site most recently
- whether the site is currently active, of only secondary interest, or dead (*)
- an overall category (e.g. staff lists, alumni, sports, public affairs, personal sites)

- a subcategory
- the name of the person mentioned on the website
- whether there is a photograph of them on the website
- the name of your own cached file of the page
- the original title of the page (Internet Explorer offers this as the file name)
- the date on which the cache copy was made
- any comment

(*) By maintaining this field, it is possible to create your own three-part web directory. It is generally most useful to sort saved hyperlinks so that there is one page of prime and active links that can be published on a website, one page of secondary links (e.g. mirror sites, repetitions of the same information) which are only likely to be of interest to you personally, and one page of dead URLs, which could link to your private cache rather than to the internet.

1.2.5.2 Book Indexes

Book Catalogues

Library catalogues contain bibliographic records that will not only reveal bearers of your study name who were authors, but also those mentioned in book titles and those who have been publishers.

It is most efficient to begin with meta-catalogues that combine the catalogues of many libraries. Currently, the most effective is **World Cat** (http://worldcat.org), which states that it lists 1 billion books in 10,000 libraries worldwide, combining OPAC databases from multiple libraries.

An online public access catalogue (OPAC) contains bibliographic records that can be searched via the internet. The biggest single OPAC databases, covering books from many countries, are those of the **Library of Congress** (Washington DC) and the **British Library** (London). The Online Catalogue to the Library of Congress (http://catalog.loc.gov) offers links to other catalogues too.

The British Library Public Catalogue (http://catalogue.bl.uk) enables a search of 12 million items in the British Library Collections, but does not include a search of 9 million periodical articles. A wider search, in multiple British libraries, is available with **Copac** (http://www.copac.ac.uk/copac/).

Online full-text search

Searches within books not only discover your study name among authors and in titles but also in the texts of the books.

The principal search mechanism currently available is the **Google Print** programme (http://books.google.com). One must register to make full use of the service, but there is no charge.

Also useful for contemporary books is the **Amazon** (http://amazon.com or http://amazon.co.uk) "Search Inside" project, which is offered as an additional search feature after calling up initial search results on that online bookshop's website. To make full use of this, you will need to have bought a book and be registered as a customer of the Amazon U.S. or British store.

Both projects employ complex strategies to prevent you printing or saving an image of the book pages. It is possible to circumvent these by using the Firefox browser. While viewing the page, open Firefox's Tools menu and choose Page Info. In the next window, choose the tab "Media" and search through the "background" images till you find the page image. This can then be saved using a name of your own choice with the extension .png, for example "chairman.png". Once you have chosen a name and location, press the "Save As..." button. Some images are deliberately made grey so that they cannot be printed, but they are legible on screen.

1.2.5.3 Indexes of Patents

Patent records contain very large numbers of surnames from multiple countries and are often a rewarding field for one-name methods, providing the names of inventors who may be scientists, engineers or in some cases untrained individuals with brilliant minds. Because patents are often registered in several countries at once, European patent records will contain many American names and vice versa. Obviously the information is not genealogical, but it is possible to establish a lot of biographical information, particularly if multiple patents are awarded to the same person.

The major database in this field is **Espacenet**, the European Patent Office gateway, at http://ep.espacenet.com/ If this is unavailable, then try the British or Irish sites, http://gb.espacenet.com/ and http://ie.espacenet.com/. Containing data on up to 60 million patent documents from around the globe, this free service is described as one of the world's biggest technology databases, and draws information from many nations' separately maintained databases. Surnames can be searched in abstracts of US patents dating back to 1920 and of British patents back to 1918.

The **US Patent and Trademark Office** has an online database with a full-text search of patents issued since 1976: http://www.uspto.gov/patft/index.html. Google has begun to create an independent OCR-based index of the US patent images for the period 1790 to 1975. Previously this period had been a blank for names researchers, because the US Patent and Trademark Office online index was searchable only by Issue Date, Patent Number, and Current US Classification, not names. This additional index can be found at: http://www.google.com/patents. You do of course have to consider the possible errors in OCR readings of your name and include common misspellings in the search.

The **UK Patent Office** also maintains databases on non-patent rights. To discover if your name forms part of a trademark, search http://www.patent.gov.uk/tm/t-find/t-find-tmtsearch/.

Pre-1918 British patents cannot yet be researched online, but many can be researched by a personal visit to the patent section of the British Library: http://www.bl.uk/patents.

1.2.5.4 Reports of Case Law

Case law is a fertile area for the one-name method, because:

- the records are indexed according to the surnames of the parties;
- the indexes are maintained at national and sometimes international level;
- the case reports often contain interesting biographical information.

Copious records of law cases are a feature of English-language jurisdictions, where legal decisions are usually guided by past cases. In other jurisdictions, decisions are more guided by principles than by jurisprudence, so the case records are sparser and less promising for one-name studies. For more information, see Wikipedia, http://en.wikipedia.org/wiki/Law_report.

In the past, law cases had to be searched using the indexes to bound volumes in law libraries. Today, the principal free source of case records is the admirable **World Legal Information Institute** (http://www.worldlii.org/), which has so far compiled a considerable stock of English and Australian case law and placed it on open access. The British part of the database is named **BAILII** and the Australian part **AustLII**. Unfortunately, other nations have yet to contribute on a similar scale to this excellent initiative.

Since full-text search is available, the results also indicate cases where a person of the surname may only have given evidence. Unfortunately, the peculiarly remote jargon of judicial opinions often leads British judges to describe witnesses as "a Mr Gibbs" or "a Mrs Smith", without disclosing that person's first name. The incidental names from full-text search may even be too copious, including lists of lawyers with the sought surname and cross-references to past cases that include the surname. However it will usually be no great task to filter out what is unnecessary to the one-name study.

There are also several fee-based databases, but the charges, oriented to the spending power of law offices, are usually prohibitive for the one-name researcher. A free search is possible at **JustCite** (http://www.justcite.com/), a legal searching engine, to indicate what full-text material can be found on leading online services including Justis, Butterworths and BAILII.

Non-lawyer users of **Westlaw** (http://www.westlaw.com/), operated by Thomson West, must offer credit card details before searching and pay for viewing. Case reports on **LexisNexis**, operated by Reed Elsevier, and on the **Casetrack** service are available only by subscription, with enormous charges for each case downloaded.

Students enrolled at university law faculties do gain preferential terms, and may be able to search the LexisNexis CaseBase case citator for you: one version of this is advertised as containing 650,000 annotations covering recent major British and Australian law reports. Commonwealth lawyers can also use Sweet and Maxwell's **Current Legal Information** (CLI), a database of law cases, some of which go back as far as 1947.

Scattered online reports and cases mentioned in commentaries can also be accessed through web search engines by a simple expedient: placing the letter v (which stands for "versus" but is pronounced "and") in front of or behind the surname sought. For example, if you are seeking the name Gibbs in cases such as Smith v Gibbs or Gibbs v Brown, do a search of *v Gibbs OR Gibbs v*. Sometimes a point is printed after the letter v, but major search engines such as Google ignore punctuation and return results that are both with and without the point.

The **Old Bailey Online** site (http://www.oldbaileyonline.org/) contains brief accounts of a large number of early criminal cases in London.

National archives also contain many court records indexed by surname. The online catalogue of the UK **National Archives** (http://www.nationalarchives.gov.uk/catalogue/) is a particularly rewarding place to hunt for case names. The **US National Archives** has only digitised a tiny part of its catalogue, but a search of the Archival Research Catalogue (**ARC**) (http://www.archives.gov/research/arc/) should be conducted.

Newspaper databases, particularly Thomson's *The Times of London* and Gale Cengages's *British Library 19th Century Newspapers*, are another good source of information on British law cases. The Times used to list all cases set down for hearing by the national courts, even if it did not report their outcomes.

When compiling a database of law cases, many of which may be mentioned by more than one source, it is advisable to make each case into a separate dataset, with the component information arranged in standard fields. Suitable fields are:

- Case Name, The First Party (Plaintiff/Appellant)
- Case Name, The Second Party (Defendant/Respondent)
- Case Name of appeals or related actions
- Year of the original legal action
- Citation (A standard abbreviation, showing where to find a case that has appeared in a law report. Some cases may have two or three citations. Note that square brackets mark a year that is at the same time a volume number. Otherwise years are in round brackets followed by the true volume number, for example: (1983) 158 CLR 1 or [1998] 2 All ER 153)
- Summary (a brief summary of the role of the person with your study name in the matter in dispute, and how they were affected by the verdict)
- Court Papers (archival reference to the judge's notes, court notebooks or documents)
- Other Papers (e.g. solicitors' correspondence involving the case from regional archives)
- Report Online (the URL of any online report of a case, for example on LII sites)
- Report in Print (a more detailed explanation of the citation above, possibly also noting which library stocks the law-report volume)
- Report in Newspapers
- Commentary (a citation of any books by legal writers mentioning the case)

1.2.5.5 Biographical Indexes

Biographical indexes, available in major academic libraries, accumulate lists of names from large numbers of biographical dictionaries and Who's Who publications. They are useful as they sometimes reveal emigrants from the trunk area for your study name.

The largest such indexing project is the **World Biographical Index** (WBI) published in Munich by K.G. Saur Verlag. It is said to contain names of 3.85 million persons worldwide. It compiles biographical articles from printed reference works published from the 16th to the 21st century, and reproduces these original documents as facsimile images on screen. The WBI is searchable online but is no longer free: web access is now syndicated by Thomson Gale to participating libraries.

A similarly ambitious project was the multi-volume Index Bio-bibliographicus Notorum Hominum (IBN) published by Biblio Verlag in the German city of Osnabrück. The printed volumes to date only cover the first few letters of the alphabet: so the IBN is useful for names such as Atwell and Bowen but not for Yelland or Zane.

The first edition of the ***Dictionary of National Biography*** is available on Ancestry at http://content.ancestry.com/iexec/?htx=List&dbid=6892. The new **Oxford DNB** is available in most large reference libraries. The online edition http://www.oxforddnb.com/ can be accessed free of charge at home with your library ticket if you live in an area where the local library service has purchased a subscription.

The ***General Biographical Dictionary*** by Alexander Chalmers. Volumes 1-32. London: J. Nichols and Son, 1812-17, is also available on Ancestry for browsing or searching, at http://content.ancestry.com/Browse/list.aspx?dbid=7077.

1.2.5.6 International newspaper indexes

Newspaper indexes take three forms:

- databases which are natively digital, having been created on computerised editorial systems since the late 1980s;
- retro projects to digitise the print newspapers that existed before that date and create full-text indexes of their content;
- hand extractions, such as *Palmer's Index to The Times*. A few such indexes continue as labours of love and interest, but the small yield for the work involved means that all of these are very tiny in scale.

Online facsimile editions of historic newspapers arrived on the internet around 2003 as broadband access made it possible to download very large files fast. Some were merely provided with a date index, but not a full-text index, making them of little practical interest to one-namers. The evolution of full-text indexes, created by using optical-character-recognition (OCR) software to scan all the pages, makes it possible to search for surnames among hundreds of millions of words.

Full-text indexes are effectively an invisible layer of machine-readable text behind the facsimile that one sees on screen. In the current generation of online databases, it is usually possible to cut and paste this text. Noting the differences between the OCR transcript and the text you see on the facsimile will help teach you what errors the software is most likely to make when it encounters damaged or smudged letters.

The Newspaper Archive, http://www.newspaperarchive.com/, is a very large and growing database, mainly of US newspapers but expanding into Canadian and British titles. When entering the website directly, you are asked to take out a subscription, but a free search is possible using Google Archive Search, (see below), which takes one to results pages with the complete OCR transcripts. It is possible to cut and paste out of these transcripts and also to see a small image of the newspaper page, allowing one to at least read the page layout and headlines, all without paying.

Google News Archive Search (http://news.google.com/archivesearch) is effectively a metasearch engine that checks multiple databases of newspapers and periodicals: it is particularly useful for mid-20th-century sources, but also embraces some 19th-century newspapers. Many of the finds are from the website Newspaper Archive (above).

LexisNexis offers an online news digest based on direct digital input from a variety of daily newspapers going back to 1984, but this is only available by an expensive subscription.

Google Alerts (http://www.google.com/alerts?hl=en) is not a searchable index, but an automatic daily scan of contemporary online newspapers for your study name. If there are any hits in this daily index, these are sent to you by email. This makes it an essential tool for biographical indexing.

Other Indexes

See also the Wiki pages for *Full-Text Newspaper Indexes* (England and Wales) as well as the Newspaper headings on the Guild Wiki pages for:

- Ireland: *Sources for Ireland*
- New Zealand: *Sources for New Zealand*
- the United States: *Sources for the USA*

1.3 Study size

When collecting data for a one-name study, it is useful to know how much data there is likely to be, or how big the study is likely to turn out. There are a number of different scales against which to measure the size of the study. For those studying a name with English/Welsh origins, one such scale is based on the number of individuals in the 1881 census of England and Wales:-

- 1-30 Tiny (T)
- 30-300 Small (S)
- 300-3000 Medium (M)
- 3000-30000 Large (L)
- 30000-300,000 Extra large (XL)
- >300,000 'Smith and Jones' (XXL)

The source of this scale is not known, but it appears to be a refinement of a system proposed by the late Geoff Riggs (*"The 1881 Surname Distribution Project – British Surname Distribution"* in *JOONS,* July 1997, Vol.6 No.3).

However, where names are mainly found outside England/Wales, this scale may not be appropriate. Not only may the name be more frequent in its country of origin, but it may in turn have expanded significantly due to migration to the New World, particularly if it originates in countries like Ireland or Germany which played such a large role in seeding the modern population of the United States.

Another disadvantage to this particular scale is that it is too coarse. Each entry covers a range which differs by a factor of 10. Thus, if a ONS with 300 people in the 1881 census would take about 10 years to complete, then one with 3000 would presumably take 100 years or more. So if I were to tell you that my study was of medium size then you wouldn't know whether I had a few years' work, or more than a lifetime's, ahead of me.

It is not even clear why anyone should want to use this particular scale, since it would appear to be easier, and more useful, simply to give the number of 1881 entries.

For example, it is estimated that the total number of BMD index entries 1837-2003 for England and Wales is about ten times the 1881 population (not exactly! but a good order of magnitude estimate). So a study with 3000 people in 1881 implies about 30,000 BMD entries to collect.

Two methods to estimate the historical number are given below (see *1.3.1: Smallshaw and Banwell methods*).

Alternative estimates may be made from present day surname frequencies. There are several useful websites where you can find estimates of the numbers of individuals with particular surnames.

- http://www.taliesin-arlein.net/names/search.php: This is based on an Office of National Statistics database covering England, Wales and the Isle of Man. The site suggests that "multiplying the result for your surname by 0.93 will give a good idea of the living population for your surname, and multiplying by 3.5 will give the population since the start of parish registers in the 16th century."
- http://www.census.gov/genealogy/www/freqnames.html – gives the frequency of names based on a sample from the 1990 US Census. Multiplying by the US population on 1st April 2000 of 281,421,906 gives an estimate comparable in date to

the previous one. However, because it is a sample of 7.2 million names from a single search area, rare surnames may easily be under- or over-represented in the sample.

- http://www.nationaltrustnames.org.uk/ – compares data based on the 1998 Great Britain Electoral Roll with the 1881 census and data from Northern Ireland (2003), Irish Republic (2003), Australia (2002), New Zealand (2002), USA (1990) and Canada (unspecified date). With some computation the relative rate of occurrence can be turned into population estimates.
- http://freepages.genealogy.rootsweb.com/~irishsurnames/index.html – gives a variety of information on Irish surnames, including frequency and main concentrations in Ireland in 1890, and data on frequency in England and Wales, Scotland and America. The Irish data is taken from Matheson's Special Report on Surnames and were estimates based on registered births in the year 1890.

1.3.1 Smallshaw and Banwell Methods

1.3.1.1 Smallshaw identification number

This is a system proposed and developed by Guild member Ronald Smallshaw (1924-1997) in the *Journal of One-Name Studies*, January 1994, Vol.5 No.1 p.12 under the heading "*Identifying a name*".

This allocated a value number to any surname in order to indicate its frequency. The method took the number of registered births in England and Wales in 1870 and 1970, and calculated the average of these two years for the county "within which the majority of births were registered".

A use of this method to classify surnames is suggested by Eric Banwell in the *Journal*, October 1996, Vol.5 No.12 pp 380-382 under the heading "*High Frequency Name Studies*".

1.3.1.2 Banwell method, index or ratio

This system was proposed and developed by Guild member Eric Banwell (1927-1998).

It was developed in order to establish the density of a surname when extracted from Phone Books (formerly Telephone Directories) and Electoral Rolls, such as are available from the 192.com website.

Guild member Philip J Sherwood (2391) described the "Banwell Ratio" thus:

The ratio is x/y divided by A/B where
x = no. of occurrences in County (or other local unit)
y = population of County
A = total no. of occurrences in census
B = population of census

Thus the global average is 1.0. The more skewed or localised is the distribution, the higher the ratio.

The book *The Surname Detective*, pub.1995, by Colin Rogers, described this method in more detail.

Unfortunately, the Banwell Index is very scale-dependent, meaning that the smaller the regions used the higher the peak value will be. The change can be dramatic, ranging from 1 when using the largest possible size of region to tens of thousands for the smallest possible size. For this reason, the regions used must be stated: counties, states, etc.

1.4 Collaborative working

Data collection can be a massive job even with a relatively small study. For larger studies, it can very usefully be shared between a number of interested researchers working collectively.

Many Guild members are experimenting with different systems of collaborative research, all of whom are convinced that teams of people can make more progress – most obviously with the data collection – than one person working alone. Collaborative working is under way in:

- Studies of high frequency surnames, which can have data collection requirements running into the hundreds of thousands in the major transcriptions.
- International studies, reflecting the multi-language requirements of surnames with large modern-day emigrant populations.
- Studies using specialised knowledge, such as combined documentary/DNA studies.

Teams can comprise people from different cultures, with different views as to how work shall be done, with differing inter-personal skills and with different tools available to them. If one is to gain optimal benefit from all the people working on data collection, a number of areas need to be addressed.

1.4.1 Working on a large study

The size of the task can influence what data is collected. However, the more people that are collecting the data, the more can be achieved in a given time. So, whilst a person addressing a "small" study (see above, *1.3: Study Size*) may be able to aim to extract all English births, deaths and marriages from the GRO in a year, one addressing an XXL study may set the aim of extracting five years' worth of data every year. A team of ten may be able to extract all the data for the XXL study in three years.

The size of the study may influence the decision as to the scope of the data collected. For example, whilst it may be feasible to record the names of spouses to "names" for a small study, doing so for an XXL study may be deemed inappropriate.

Team communication

As the data collection progresses, there are numerous reasons why the various people need to communicate – examples include letting the other members of the team know how one is progressing and asking for help. Another example is especially relevant for the longer term collection exercise.

Where data collection takes a significant time – years, decades or even generations – it is important to consider how to ensure that the collection stays on track and that new team members can join with the minimum of disruption and start bringing their efforts to bear as soon as possible. One approach is to use newsletters which can not only allow team members to share the ups and downs of the work (it can be seen as a lonely, unrewarding and frustrating task) but also form a permanent record of such as:

- progress made
- assumptions used
- where the resulting data is
- problems to be overcome
- updated techniques / tools
- plans for the coming months

With the various members of the team having different technologies available to them, the team may need to be able to communicate using a number of channels. For example, some could be using letters, others email, some voice (e.g. audio tape or telephone). The team needs to consider the most appropriate methods to be used for each task.

Data collation

At some stage, the results of the data collection need to be brought together to support the future stages of the one-name study. The team should not wait for the collection to be complete as this could take many years and benefits could be gained from the data gathered to date.

With data being collected in various formats, on different media and to different standards, a way should be found to create a single collection. However, this does not necessarily mean having all the data in one place. For example – databases can be linked, documents can be copied.

Summary

These are just some of the issues that should be addressed in order to benefit from more than one person carrying out data collection. It has by no means covered them all, and has not addressed each in any depth. However, it is hoped that it has helped pose questions that, when addressed, may help people with their study.

1.5 Overcoming index errors

1.5.1 Handwriting difficulties

Human indexing of handwritten documents is often handicapped by unclear handwriting in the originals. While mistranscriptions of census returns and similar documents are frustrating, every researcher should treat them as ultimately useful clues and carefully record the errors to compile a table of the most likely misreadings of "their" name.

This can then be used in future searches of the index when an exact-spelling search proves fruitless. For example:

- Blackwell was found in the Ancestry.com index of the 1901 England census as "Blacknall"
- Pepys was found in the Ancestry.com index of the 1900 US Federal census as "Peeper", "Peepo", "Pups"
- Bliss was found in the Ancestry.com index of the 1891 England census as "Blias" and "Blies"
- Cosser was found in the Ancestry.com index of the 1851 England census as "Eoper" and in the 1861 as "Copes"

Handwriting errors can also be transmitted to printed indexes where they are more challenging to spot. For example, where some of the early England and Wales GRO indexes were retyped in the 1960s, the old long SS (ß) was transcribed as P, turning Cossentine into Copentine, yet retaining the original alphabetical position. It is worthwhile rechecking your BMD index extractions on FreeBMD, viewing the original images and giving extra scrutiny to those entries which appear to be out of sequence. In this way 40 "new" entries were found for a relatively small but mature study with 3900 entries in England and Wales.

1.5.2 OCR

While one-name research primarily uses indexes compiled by clerks, transcription teams or professional indexers, every study will have to make some use of full-text indexes that are the product of automated optical character recognition (OCR), which is the most economical way of processing printed sources.

OCR indexes are compiled by scanning photographic copies of the original documents and "reading" every character of every line of visible text to create a somewhat imperfect character-by-character version of the document. Software then seeks meaningful words in the text string to compile an index of the document.

Even at the scanning stage, some words will be unrecognisable because of spots on the paper, worn or dirty type used to print the original, broken type and typesetting and editing errors in the original. The OCR software will then fail to match many characters with stored patterns. To demonstrate why this is so, the British Library has published examples of the poor state of many of the newspapers in its collection.

Most databases will also filter out all illogical words, for example those in which the small letter L has been erroneously replaced by the digit 1. Some providers attempt to correct such words by finding the most likely matches in a dictionary, others just delete them.

1.5.3 Search strategies

When searching, it is often possible to increase your hit rate by trying for look-alike readings. This is particularly useful in searches of the London, Edinburgh and Belfast Gazettes at the http://www.gazettes-online.co.uk site. For example, enter "Giirney" (where the U is replaced by two letters I) and you find Lieutenant J. Gurney. "Skegncss" with a C finds Skegness. "Sniith" finds up to 12 instances of Smith.

Obsolete letters should also be checked in other guises, for example names that include an S or double-S should be sought using transcriptions in which a long S is replaced by a lower-case F, P or FS.

If you are searching for a name beginning with C, try G as well, and vice versa, even in printed indexes.

While the Gazettes Online database only allows wildcard searches that truncate from the right, the Thomson Gale index search to The Times allows wildcard characters in the middle of words. These can be used in combination with a Boolean search. For example, after doing a first search for "HEMPSALL", one might do a second search for "HEM*S*L NOT HEMPSALL". Some of the hits might then seem illogical, for example one of the returned results is "TAKE PLACE , THERE IS NO". However this would be logically correct if the OCR software had only slightly misread the original text as "TAKE PLACE , THEM IS LO".

1.6 Organising your data

Your collected data may include all the following types:

- Genealogical data (vital records)
- Other text based material
- Images
- Sound
- Video

The following storage media might be considered:

- Paper, including parchment, vellum and record cards
- Magnetic – disks (floppy, Zip, hard) and tape
- Semi-conductor, e.g. flash memory sticks
- Optical: film and fiche
- Optical disks: CD-ROM, DVD-ROM

Two important points about all media:

- All types of media become obsolete (but paper, especially acid-free paper, is doing well!)
- All media degrade

Methods of storing and recording:

- Record cards and paper
- Word processors
- Spreadsheets
- Databases
- 'Family Tree' programs (lineage-linked databases)
- Specialised databases, e.g Custodian, Clooz
- Desk-top publishing
- The worldwide web

Many of the above use proprietary data formats, so when exchanging information with others, consider using:

- GEDCOM for lineage-linked data
- For text, use plain text (.TXT), rich text format (.RTF) or portable document format (.PDF)
- For databases and spreadsheets, comma or tab separated variables (.CSV or .TSV)
- For pictures, many formats exist. Best options are TIF, JPG and GIF.

Consider using a desktop search engine on your computer in order to locate all those facts stored in miscellaneous files and emails.

With a large amount of information to store, it becomes necessary to have systems for linking the stored information to particular people and families. This usually involves lineage reconstruction (see *3.3: Lineage reconstruction* below). It will also require you to devise an adequate system of naming the various families and lineages that you discern in your data.

1.6.1 Systems of naming

Collating genealogical information on unrelated families requires some form of lineage labelling system to assist in organising your data, allow quick searching and data retrieval, and allow others to communicate easily with you about which lineage they are referring to. Many one-namers have a system that was developed when their study was in an early stage and has then evolved over the years. The systems in use therefore vary with the nature of the study, particularly with study size and geographical distribution. No one system suits all, but there are some common approaches in use. In the examples given below, it may be worth looking at the websites for these studies (where they exist) to see the methods in action.

Numbering of family trees or family group sheets

- Using numbers starting at 1 is the obvious approach. But if you have many trees, the approach used in the **Crabbe** ONS may be useful. Here the trees are numbered from 101, so that all trees have three digits, which is advantageous when the number is converted to text by a computer, as leading zeroes are not lost, and sorting is consistent.

- Using single letters allows up to 26 trees which may be sufficient for a small or medium study. Following the letter with digits can allow branches, generations or individuals to be identified. Examples include:

    - the **Duncalf** ONS where each tree has a letter and every individual within a tree has a number, assigned consecutively on being linked to the tree.

    - the **Godson** ONS uses letters for particular geographical areas and the charts on which the family appears are designated by additional letters indicating period, with numbers for multiple charts in each period. For example Chart YA1 is for the family from York for 1600-1750, and this reference is indicated in the database entry for each individual on that chart.

    - the **Hempsall** ONS uses a numbering system for branches alternating adding letters and numbers, but only when inheritance of the name forks into more than one branch; even with 14 generations only six components are needed to give branch labels of the form: 4C(ii)a1A.

    - the **Whillans** ONS uses a letter followed by a "Henry number" (see the Henry System at http://www.saintclair.org/numbers/numhenry.html).

- using single characters 0-9 and A-Z allows up to 36 trees, and suits single character 'flags' in genealogical databases, this is the approach used in the **Bodimeade** ONS.

- the **Bawtree** ONS uses a number for each family group, adding consecutive numbers as research establishes new groups. This method works well for a small study.

"Special" letters or numbers may be used to indicate groups which are not lineages, but for which it is convenient to have a lineage-type label. For example, the USA Duncalfs not linked to a UK lineage are all given a lineage name 'T', and individuals in the Bodimeade database not related to any Bodimeade are assigned a lineage label of "0" (zero) to distinguish them from those who are not (yet) assigned to a lineage.

Geographical labels

These may or may not use a consistent geographical unit as the basis for the labelling.

- From the place of origin or place of long term residence of the families, e.g., the 'Kent **Hollyers**' and the 'Coventry **Hollyers**'.

- The places of the marriages of a small number of couples who are ancestors of all subsequent bearers of the name. This is the approach of the **Pepperdine** ONS.

- Using parishes in areas of high concentration of the name and counties elsewhere, as is done by the **Gullick** ONS.

- By county and a number, e.g., '**Iredale** family YKS/15', sometimes with addition of the source, e.g. 'Iredale family CUL/IGI 5'. Families that are later found to have moved between counties can be accommodated with a simple addition without any restructuring, to give forms such as 'CUL~LAN/7' indicating movement from Cumberland to Lancashire.

For small studies where the majority of bearers of the name lived in a very few places, geographical labels are not useful.

Founder labels

These are based on the name(s) at the head of the tree.

- The **Fidler** ONS uses the maiden name of the wife at the top of the tree.

- The **Pobjoy** ONS uses the forename of the husband and the maiden name of the wife at the top of the tree, e.g. William/LEE.

This method has the disadvantage of changing the labels every time a new generation is added, but for small or medium studies, as research becomes more complete they stabilise and change rarely.

Combined number, geographical and/or name labels

- County or country followed by name at the head of the tree, e.g. 'USA Job'.

- by country, county or state, start date and submitter, e.g. 'England, Suffolk, Shimpling, 1546, John Smith'. This method is used by the **Steed-Stead** ONS and is particularly well suited for the nature of large and extra-large studies. Trees arrived at by collaborative work are not given a submitter name, but are labelled with a date for the version, so the label is of the form 'Steads of Kent, Ramsgate, 2006'. This has the advantage that if an error is found one can revert to the previous version and rebuild from there.

- The **Bandy** ONS uses names for lineages of the form 'Joseph (D0694-1724) Padstow' comprising founder name, identification number, approximate date of birth and location. Within the identification number the letter represents which of the two principal researchers is dealing with the line, and the number is unique to the individual.

Distinctive characteristics

Any distinctive characteristic of the family, e.g. the 'post-office **Heveys**' or a distinctive variant spelling. This may seem unsystematic, but works because the labels have clear meanings and are easily recalled.

Methods not recommended

One method which is reported to have been good initially, but to have caused problems in the long run, is to name lineages after correspondents who are researching the lines. As the number of contacts grows, this method becomes unwieldy.

Other aspects of naming lineages

For the **Rowberry** ONS, an additional help with organising data is the colour coding of the families. The colours can then be applied to folders for paper records or web pages. They are even used for name badges at family gatherings so that distant cousins can easily recognise each other, which they all find greatly helpful and much fun!

Within lineages there are numerous approaches to labelling generations. Some one-namers use numbering schemes, whilst others continue to use geographical labels, or a combination of the two. At the level of individuals, numbering within a lineage is possible, or using names associated with generation labels, e.g. the form used in the **Medlock** ONS is Tempsford Generation X (maiden surname) – MDX, which follows the geographical name for the lineage with a generation number, qualified by the mother's maiden name and the place they migrated to from Tempsford. Others, such as the **Bodimeade** ONS, number individuals independently of lineage, so the individual's number does not change with their assignment (or lack of assignment) to a lineage. Richard Pence, on his website http://www.saintclair.org/numbers/, has given a general account of numbering systems in use in genealogy with their pros and cons.

2. Analysis

2.1 How to analyse your documentary data

There are several levels at which your analysis takes place:

1. Ensuring that each piece of data you have researched is as complete as possible.
2. Linking each piece of data to the correct individual name bearer in your study.
3. Linking individual name bearers in your study to the correct family group or tree.
4. Using the results of your analysis in levels 1-3 to draw conclusions about your name and generate a set of hypotheses by which you can test new data.

2.1.1 Data completion

This can be a very time-consuming task, but it is worth doing. In some cases it requires you to use other features of a website hosting the data you've collected to build up a fuller picture of the data. In other cases it requires you to search the website you're using in a wider way.

Examples:

- Marriage entries in the FreeBMD indexes online show only the spouse's maiden name. However, by clicking on the entry reference you can call up all the other entries under it, one of which should be the first name of the spouse.

- Census transcription indexes always contain a proportion of surnames indexed incorrectly. Within your own study you need to not only make a list of likely 'variant' spellings (i.e. legitimate variations of your study name), but also the most common 'deviant' spellings (i.e. invented spellings which were never used by their holders). Between them these two strategies will identify at least some of the otherwise 'missing data' potentially lost through mis-transcription. Note that the kind of wildcard searches allowed in the surname field will vary between websites.

2.1.2 Linking data to the correct individual

As you collect data from different sources and of differing classes, you'll begin to link them together to form profiles of individual name bearers. The aim here is that each new piece of data added to a profile will both corroborate the profile and expand it. To achieve that in many cases you'll find yourself trying to fill in a missing fact by searching across multiple data sources.

2.1.3 Linking each individual to the correct family group and tree

This follows on from the activity in *2.1.2: Linking data to the correct individual*, above. Census material is especially useful here as it groups individuals into families. Collecting material from a range of censuses is the most efficient way to group the majority of individuals within the correct family group.

2.1.4 Generating testable hypotheses

The more data you collect, the more difficult it becomes for patterns in the data to emerge unaided. Further, as the matching and linking processes described above progress, the questions you have remaining will become more and more specific; for example, do these two trees which appear to originate in adjoining parishes actually form part of a single tree? It is easier to resolve this type of question by formulating a question of your own, your hypothesis, to ask the data. Even if the answer is not clear, by setting that reference point you will notice as new data comes in whether it has inclined you towards agreeing or disagreeing with your hypothesis.

2.1.5 Family reconstruction

Collectively, the actions outlined in *2.1.2* – *2.1.4* above are known as family reconstruction or lineage reconstruction, building up a composite picture of the trees within a surname by using data from different classes and origins. Family reconstitution is a more practical goal for medium and small studies than large ones, and your strategy to perform it varies according to study size.

2.1.6 Study conclusions

By creating linked data you have opened up the opportunity to synthesise it in various ways. This is covered in more detail in *3: Synthesis*, below. There is the potential (so far not explored within the Guild) to compare data across different surname studies.

2.2 Using maps

Maps are important tools for several aspects of one-name studies. Their uses include:

- As aids to locating ancestors perhaps in conjunction with gazetteers
- As aids to research and data collection
- To analyse the distribution of the name, an important part of ***analysis***
- To present data, investigations, and subsequent results, in publications and for displays, part of your work on ***synthesis*** and ***publication of results***.

Three sorts of map can be distinguished:

- Published maps (on paper, on CD or online)
- Self-produced maps
- Maps generated by programs (on CD or online) using your own data, or studied name, as input

2.2.1 Locating ancestors using maps

When trying to identify the location of any of your families, it's important to find a map that is contemporary to the time of your data; the growth of towns, particularly during the 19th and 20th centuries, meant major changes. In Britain villages were absorbed into towns and street names changed. Gazetteers, especially contemporary ones, may assist. Trade Directories, many now published on CD, provide more background information on places.

If the name of the place hasn't changed, then many modern day interactive online maps can assist location. These include:

- Google Maps US – http://maps.google.com/
- Google Maps UK – http://maps.google.co.uk/
- Streetmap – http://www.streetmap.co.uk

Other resources are listed in *2.2.3: Sources of Maps*, below.

2.2.2 Gazetteers

In order to locate ancestors, it is often necessary to understand place names as they were used at the time, as well as where these places fall today (which may assist finding where their records are kept). Useful resources include:

- Ordnance Survey Gazetteer
- ABC Gazetteer from the Association of British Counties
- The Genuki Gazetteer
- UK Placename Finder from Archaeology UK

Much more than a Gazetteer is Vision of Britain (http://www.visionofbritain.org.uk/index.jsp) which provides useful information about UK administrative units both now and in the past.

2.2.3 Sources of maps

There are many sources of maps. These can be used as they are for information purposes, but can often also be used as a basis for creating your own maps, by scanning hard copies, or by saving electronic versions.

Hard copies:

- Atlases, e.g. Phillimore's Atlas of UK parishes
- Road maps
  - AA Auto maps
  - Rand McNally (North America)
- Ordnance Survey or North America Topographic maps

On CD:

- Atlases (e.g. the "Find your way around..." series)
- Historic Parishes of England and Wales (http://ahds.ac.uk/history/collections/hpew.htm), a definitive and detailed set of maps showing parish boundaries c. 1850
- Various maps for UK and abroad from Archive CD Books (http://www.archivecd-books.org/)

Historic maps

- Cassini maps (http://www.cassinimaps.co.uk/shop)
- Your Old Books and Maps Online (http://www.yourbooksonline.co.uk/)
- The Godfrey Edition old Ordnance Survey maps (http://www.alangodfreymaps.co.uk/)

Map portals

- Map History/Cartography (http://www.maphistory.info/imagebi.html)
- Your Maps on line (http://www.yourmapsonline.org.uk)
- Oddens bookmarks (http://oddens.geog.uu.nl/index.php)
- MOTCO (http://www.motco.com)
- David Rumsey Map Collection (http://www.davidrumsey.com/index.html) – Over 20,000 18th and 19th century maps which can be scrutinised online or downloaded.

Other finding aids:

- Online use –
    - Streetmap (http://www.streetmap.co.uk)
    - Bing maps, formerly Multimap (http://www.bing.com)
    - Google Maps (http://maps.google.com/)
    - Virtual Earth, Microsoft's competitor to Google Maps and Google Earth (http://local.live.com). Both can be used to create bespoke maps for your one-name study, by adding 'push-pins'.
    - Ordnance Survey Get-a-Map (http://www.ordnancesurvey.co.uk/oswebsite/getamap/)
    - Old Maps UK Ordnance Survey maps circa 1880 (http://www.old-maps.co.uk/)
    - MOTCO online maps of old London (http://www.motco.com)
    - David Rumsey Map Collection Over 20,000 18th and 19th century maps which can be scrutinised online or downloaded (http://www.davidrumsey.com/)
    - Many of the Genuki parish pages (http://www.genuki.org.uk/) also include links to relevant maps (as probably do the Genweb pages).
    - Neighbourhood Statistics and Maps Official UK government data (http://neighbourhood.statistics.gov.uk/dissemination/)

- Downloadable –
    - Parloc or Parish Locator: free downloadable software in several versions, available from http://web.onetel.net.uk/~gdlawson/parfind.htm or http://parloc.pwp.blueyonder.co.uk/ParLocDL.html
    - Google Earth: a free downloadable program but then used with an online (broadband) connection

2.2.4 Publishing old maps

If you have old maps, you can integrate them with modern electronic maps by adding them as layers. This also helps to add "geo-references" of latitude and longitude to your place data. If you then publish the maps online, search engines may be able to direct users to your site with the help of geographic search terms.

Be aware that early maps may be only schematic and may not match well with aerial photographs and modern maps. Nevertheless, it can be very useful to see them layered.

A sophisticated example is Donald Rumsey's modern re-edition of an 1843 London street map at the Rumsey pages (http://rumsey.geogarage.com/maps/g0890184.html), which uses Google Maps as a background layer. Use the transparency slider to make the 1843 map semi-transparent and compare the aerial photos or the Google Map as background.

The following procedure uses Google Earth, but can be employed with other software as well:

1. Scan the maps and save them in one of the usual graphic formats. Scanning the map in sections is often more practical and results in more manageable file sizes.
2. Open Google Earth and click the “layer” button at the top to make a new layer.
3. Load the picture file into this new layer, either by dragging it or using the “load” button.
4. Reduce the transparency of this new layer to about half, using the slider control in the navigation bar (at the left).
5. Rotate and resize the scanned map to fit the group in the aerial photograph below it.

You can then use push pins to mark locations of interest, for example of farms or old houses, on the old-new map.

If the map is in the public domain and you are certain there are no copyright issues, you may also want to consider publishing this geo-referenced version online to assist other researchers. The following procedure can be used to publish a Google Earth map in Google Maps, a different service offered by the Google company:

1. Right-click on the new layer in the left panel listing layers, and use “Save Place as...” in the context menu to save this as a .KMZ file.
2. Upload the KMZ file to a host server that you control somewhere on the internet.
3. After checking that the file is accessible, paste the URL of your KMZ file into the Google Maps search box and click Search. Your map will appear as an image layered on the appropriate Google Maps image or street map.
4. Although the rotation and transparency will not have been transferred to Google Maps, you can still adjust the zoom level on the Google Maps site.
5. Click on the “Link” (to this page) link that appears in the top-right corner of the page.
6. Copy the highlighted “Email” link from the pop-up that appears (using Ctrl+c in Windows).
7. Insert this link in your own website.

Visitors to your site will now be able to call up your scanned map with correct scaling and geo-referencing in Google Maps. If they have Google Earth installed, they will also be able to open this so as to see the map correctly tilted and made semi-transparent.

An alternative approach is employed on the maps of the Charles Booth Archive (http://booth.lse.ac.uk/), allowing comparison between late 19th London streets and the modern layout in adjoining panels. With either approach, you will need to consider dividing very large maps up into tiles so that they download to a user’s computer quickly.

2.2.5 Creating your own maps

Production methods

- Hand drawn maps
- Hand/pin marking on pre-printed or published maps (See *2.2.3: Sources of maps* above)
- Program generated maps – like Steve Archer’s **Surname Atlas** and **GenMap** programs

Styles of maps

- Simple point map – pinpoints places of interest
- Multiple symbol point map – different symbols allow for different categories of places to be shown
- Area fill – areas, e.g. parishes, counties, postcode districts, etc., are "filled in", or coloured depending on given totals. These can be actual numbers of entries, or totals in relation to other totals such as the overall population – see *2.3: Statistics for distributions*, below.
- Proportional symbol map – combines the advantages of the simple point map and the area-fill in that individual points are sized according to the number of events there.

Both the method of production, and the style of map produced, will be determined by whether the map is for private use or public display, and on what the actual purpose of the map is.

Specific examples to illustrate some of the purposes such maps can be used:

- As an aid to research and data collection
  - Area fill of counties for which a whole census has been collected
  - Area fill of Registration Districts that civil registration has been collected from
  - Points / named parishes for which parish registers have been searched
- To display data that has been collected, in order to assist in its analysis
  - To plot distributions – where all of the people with a certain surname were at a particular time, showing concentrations of name
  - To show where a particular individual lived at various / specific times of their life
  - To show different places that may have been of relevance to a person or family
  - Time series to show migration of the surname or its variants
  - Family reconstruction
  - A web page interface where data is linked to maps (See, for example, the Dangerfield Atlas, http://www.members.shaw.ca/hdangerfield/)
- To investigate issues arising from the data:
  - Relationships between clusters of the people and their occupations

Getting your data ready for mapping

Considering the possible use of maps at an early stage in the study will enable the data collected to be arranged in appropriate formats. Not all the data collected will have sufficient geographical information initially to enable mapping, so additional fields/columns might be required for coordinates (OS references, longitude and latitude etc), as well as enabling standardised versions of place names or registration districts to be included.

Although it is possible to produce simple maps based on information stored in text documents or spreadsheets, most mapping will require the ability to analyse data and to carry out queries on it. As such, databases (e.g. Access, Custodian) would be the preferred format for storage.

Issues to consider when working with maps

- Boundary changes (both whether the mapping program fits the data date wise and the issue of census counties versus geographical counties).
- Specific county problems (e.g. Yorkshire – three Ridings and York, or the whole county? GenMap and Birdie treat them differently).
- Scales of maps and how plotting at different scales can affect the picture produced.
- Whether to plot from original data or extracted totals. Original data might produce a more accurate picture, but could be time consuming, especially if plotting at parish level and some parishes are not recognised by the software. Being able to input totals for areas is necessary if plotting relative figures for distributions.

2.2.6 Program generated maps

Most mapping programs allow you to plot information about your name, either by inputting data you already have (such as IGI entries) or by inputting the surname to generate a distribution map.

Programs on CD or downloadable

- **Surname Atlas** plots surname and first name data from the 1881 census. Available from the Guild Sales Manager (see http://www.one-name.org/cgi-bin/software/sales.cgi). This is the simplest tool to use to demonstrate a surname distribution in Great Britain and is regularly demonstrated at Fairs attended by the Guild. Even non-genealogists can get hooked! The program can display at County or Poor Law Union level, using absolute numbers or relative frequency. Full details of the program can be found at Archer Software (http://www.archersoftware.co.uk).
- **GenMap** generates distribution maps using your own data. The program has an inbuilt gazetteer of parish and registration district names, thereby easing the import of your data. Full program details at Archer Software as above.
- **Agis:** shareware mapping and GIS shareware package for Windows available from http://www.agismap.com/index.html.
- **MapInfo:** see http://www.mapinfo.com – probably beyond the requirements of most genealogists!

Online programs:

- **Hamrick Software** plots densities of the 50,000 most commonly occurring names in the United States, derived from data at four specific dates.
- All US surnames are covered by a similar service offered by **Gens**, but the date the map relates to is not stated. You can then order the map on a t-shirt ... !
- **Ancestry Family Facts** plots distributions of your study name based on the 1891 England & Wales census, and from three US censuses.
- **Surname Profiler** plots the top 25,000 surnames in Britain as at 1881 and 1998.
- For names in France, distribution maps can be generated online at **La France de votre Nom De Famille**. Enter a surname to get a map showing numbers and distribution of births 1891-1915. By selecting a department, you get a list of communes where the surname appears.
- For the Netherlands, the Database of Surnames in the Netherlands (**Nederlandse Familienamen Databank**) will provide a map showing the numbers to be found in each province in the 1947 census.
- Surnames in Italy may be plotted using **L'Italia dei cognomi**. This service is part of Gens. As with their USA maps the date is not specified and you can buy the t-shirt.

- **Surname distribution analysis** requires submission of your own data, which is then plotted as a distribution map based on either the pre-1974 UK counties or the US States.
- **Karte zum Namen** gives the distribution of names in Germany based on telephone directories. Enter a name and select 'Suchen' to generate a map. Rolling the mouse over a region gives its name.

2.3 Statistics for distributions

The first question to ask is "Distribution of what?"

Let's say that you want to look at the distribution of the surname SMITHBLOGGINS. Do you want the distribution of the **number** of SMITHBLOGGINSs or of the **proportion of the population** who are called SMITHBLOGGINS?

Depending upon the source of information you are using, either quantity could be the easier one to find. If this is the wrong quantity for you then either you will need to put in a lot of extra work or you will need to use a different source. Do not let the source determine the question; let the question determine the source.

The **number** of SMITHBLOGGINS in an area will normally depend upon the population: we could expect to find more SMITHBLOGGINS in London than in the middle of the Sahara desert. In Britain, since the major cities of London, Birmingham, Coventry, Manchester, Liverpool and Glasgow lie approximately along a line going from SE to NW, counting numbers will tend to show a SE/NW trend for most names. This difficulty, which distorts – sometimes very badly – any genealogical distributions, does not exist for proportions.

There are too many difficulties when it comes to interpreting distributions of **numbers**, even though they might be very easy to produce and give pretty maps. From the genealogical point of view, the **proportion** is the more important quantity.

To find the proportion of the population of an area who are SMITHBLOGGINS, all that is needed is a source for which the following two quantities are known or can be estimated:

(a) The total number of entries
(b) The number of SMITHBLOGGINS entries.

Dividing (b) by (a) then gives the approximate proportion of SMITHBLOGGINSs in that area. Since the result will be an extremely small fraction, it is usual to quote results "the other way up", that is (a) divided by (b), as "1 in ...", e.g. "1 in 10,000". There is no need for great precision, here; if the arithmetic happens to work out at, say, 1 in 9876 then it is pointless using that number – just call it 1 in 10,000.

There is one other property needed of the source: the proportion of SMITHBLOGGINSs in the source should be the same (at least, approximately) as in the population as a whole. If this is not the case, then the source is biased, either against or in favour of SMITHBLOGGINS. For example, telephone directory entries might be biased against the poorer members of society since telephones cost money which poor people might not be able to afford. So are people called SMITHBLOGGINS known to be significantly poorer than the population as a whole? If so, then telephone directories will be biased against SMITHBLOGGINS, and so, depending upon how serious the bias is, it might not be appropriate to use telephone directories to map the distribution of SMITHBLOGGINS. Research has in fact shown that telephone entries today show a bias the other way, because richer people tend to go ex-directory and so are not shown in the figures. This bias is greater in south-eastern Britain than in other parts of the country.

The question here often confuses people and takes us into the philosophy of statistics. You do not have to know that there is no bias. That is, you do not have to set about proving that there is no bias before you can use the source. It is simply that you shouldn't be aware that there is a bias for/against your study name; ignorance on your part is fine. You don't have to worry about whether the SMITHBLOGGINSs are significantly poorer, on average, than the rest of the population (and so are likely to be significantly under-represented in telephone directories) – you may proceed on the assumption that they're not, unless you happen to know otherwise.

In practice, property (a) – the total number of entries in the source – can be difficult to find, in which case it will be necessary to estimate it. If the source is divided into a known number of relatively small sections then this is best done by counting the average number of entries in a random sample of sections (as many as you can manage before boredom sets in) and then multiplying by the number of sections. For example, staying with telephone directories, we could take a "section" as being a page: count the average number of entries per page in a random sample of pages and then multiply by the number of pages in the directory.

Another way of finding the proportion of SMITHBLOGGINS is by taking advantage of someone else's work on another surname: let's say, on the name BLOGGINSSMITH. If the BLOGGINSSMITH researcher has said that the 20 BLOGGINSSMITH entries in a particular source represent 6% of the total number of entries, and you know that the same source contains 30 SMITHBLOGGINS entries then it isn't hard to see that SMITHBLOGGINS represents 9% of the entries in that source. As a variation, the BLOGGINSSMITH researcher might not have said how many BLOGGINSSMITH entries there are, but might have given merely the percentage; in which case there is nothing to stop you from counting the number of BLOGGINSMITHs for yourself, and thus finding out that there are 20. Alternatively, of course, you could just ask.

For early systems with relevance to surname frequencies: see *1.3.1: Smallshaw and Banwell methods* above. See also the article *Methods of estimating surname frequency and distribution*, by Keith Percy in *JOONS*, January 1998, Vol.6 No.5.

Surname frequency information is also available at the following:

- http://www.britishsurnames.co.uk/
- http://www.census.gov/genealogy/www/freqnames.html
- http://worldnames.publicprofiler.org

2.4 Estimating lineage numbers

A useful report from a Guild member is included here:

Chandler ONS – How many lineages for an occupational surname?

Estimating the likely number of distinct lineages may be useful as part of a DNA study, or simply to get an idea of how many separate genealogical lineages there might be. There are a number of different approaches that can be taken, making differing assumptions.

Two approaches are illustrated here for the surname CHANDLER. A minority descend from one or more LE CHAUNDELERs who came over from Normandy around 1200. Most CHANDLERs descend from people occupied in candle-making who gained their surname in the period when hereditary surnames became common in England. By the time the Black Death had had its effect, the population of England in 1350 was down to about 2.5M. This is also about the time that surnames became hereditary (though there is much variation). Using the population totals from the 19th century English censuses, and counts of CHANDLERs from the indexes to them, and assuming the same proportion of the population bore the surname in 1350, we can calculate the same counts for 1350 and use these to estimate the number of lineages.

Year:	1851	1881	1350
England population (Note 1)	16.8m	35.5m	2.5m
CHANDLER (Note 2)	6,389	9,487	Predict 950 or 972
CHANDLER heads of household (Note 2)	1,289	2,045	Predict 192 or 210

Note 1: Population figures from Wikipedia.
Note 2: 1851 and 1881 counts are from Ancestry indexes for exact spelling Chandler only. A full analysis would add in the variants of Chandler, so the totals would be raised somewhat.

The heads of household calculation assumes that the demographic structure of the household was unchanged from the 14th to 19th centuries, but this is probably a good first approximation and much easier than trying to work out the impact of change in structure on the calculations. The two 19th century census indexes have different advantages and disadvantages: family structures are probably less changed in 1851 as there was somewhat less industrialisation, but the transcription accuracy of the 1881 index is significantly higher, so it is difficult to say which is better.

Working from the predicted total CHANDLER population of about 960 in 1350, then assuming a 50/50 sex ratio, there would be roughly 480 male CHANDLERs in 1350. Assuming that 10% of these descend from a single Norman LE CHAUNDELER (or several related ones) and his (their) descendants during those 150 years, then around 430 got their surname from the chandlery trade. To estimate the number of genetically distinct CHANDLER lines there were, that figure needs to be divided by the number of males in a typical household. A crude assumption that they were in nuclear households with a couple and an average of two-point-something children alive, leads to an estimate of less than 215 CHANDLER households.

The estimate of roughly 200 CHANDLER heads of household is very similar to that from the total population assuming a nuclear family, which gives us more confidence in the figures. These numbers give an upper limit to the number of genetically distinct lines. A chandlery might well be populated by an older male and some of his sons, together with their sons, which would make this an overestimate, and even separate chandleries might be run by paternally related individuals because the trade probably ran in families. Even if 10% are descendants of one LE CHAUNDELER, and half the rest are related to the other half, there must be at least 90 distinct lineages.

One factor which has not been considered is the extinction of lineages: some of those households in 1350 will have had only daughters, or only grand-daughters, and therefore will not have male line descendants today. Conversely there will have been non-paternity events which introduced new Y-chromosome lineages into the CHANDLER surname.

The process is rough and ready, but it appears that we can be fairly confident that the CHANDLER DNA project should expect ultimately to find of the order of 100-200 Y-chromosome lineages. The June 2008 count of genetically distinct lineages discovered by the DNA project is 54.

A third way to measure a surname's population in the late 14th century is to use the 1377-81 Poll Taxes as a form of enumeration. The full set of surviving returns is published in three volumes by Carolyn Fenwick *"The Poll Taxes of 1377, 1379 and 1381"* (British Academy and Oxford University Press, 1998, 2001, 2005), but as it is not indexed by surname there is quite a lot of work to do to find all the entries for a particular surname. (Some of these are now on Google Books but may still require manual searching!). The CHANDLER entries in this resource – a smaller number than was expected – have been extracted and analysed. As a result, taking account of the areas not included in Dr. Fenwick's work, and necessarily making many assumptions, the estimate of genetically distinct CHANDLER lineages is currently 150.

2.5 DNA Projects

One-namers now have access to a completely new set of data to augment their documentary data: Y-chromosome DNA test results.

DNA testing became available to genealogists in 2000 and is today increasingly being used by Guild members within their one-name studies in parallel with the traditional activities of oral and documentary research. As of mid-2010 an estimated 220 members, roughly 10% of Guild members, have registered a surname-defined DNA project.

Finding DNA results

It is possible to search the databases of the DNA testing companies to see if anyone has registered a Y-chromosome surname project bearing your registered surname(s), or if any name-bearer has taken a DNA test. The websites to check are:

- Family Tree DNA, both the surname search (http://www.familytreedna.com) and the surname project lists (http://www.familytreedna.com/projects.aspx)
- DNA Ancestry (http://dna.ancestry.com), a service of Ancestry.com
- Ysearch (http://www.ysearch.org/), the public database of results sponsored by Family Tree DNA

After building up a picture of what has already been done relating to your registered surname(s), your first step should be to register your study name(s) within a DNA surname project at each of the three vendors listed above. Your priority should be to register with Family Tree DNA, which makes a realistic claim to host 90% of all Y-chromosome surname projects currently being run worldwide.

Help with your DNA project

Members who are interested in setting up a DNA project as part of their one-name study can email the special Guild DNA Helpline at DNA@one-name.org to request advice and assistance. This can help you save time and avoid some of the pitfalls that are hard to anticipate as you start out. One key point needs to be emphasised: you do not need any specialist genetic or statistical knowledge to run a DNA surname project. It is a simple matter in almost all cases to accurately interpret the results in the format that they are delivered to project members, and more experienced Guild members are within email reach to help you every stage of the way.

Members using the DNA Helpline will receive the following:

- Advice on choosing the most appropriate vendor to register your project with.
- Setting up a project profile and web site tailored to your project, which you can then edit as you wish

- A step by step "getting started" email that gives you:
  - Advice on how to find others with your study name, get them to join your project and take the test
  - An easy-to-follow 11-step guide
  - Information on any promotions that could benefit your project
  - Help setting up your Guild web profile
- In the case where your Guild surname(s) have already been registered as surname DNA project(s), the DNA helpline can help you in your discussions with the administrators of the existing project to ensure data from it is shared with you
- A template recruiting email letter you can tweak and send to potential test takers
- Other recruiting help, including ways to approach people on the telephone
- Templates to help you project manage your DNA study

There are some very informative pages in the Guild Wiki listing books and articles on DNA, the "deep history" it can reveal, and various aspects of DNA testing and analysis.

2.5.1 Choosing a DNA testing company

A Y-DNA project is best managed within a surname project. Although Y-DNA tests are available from a number of testing companies, only two companies currently offer project management facilities:

- DNA Ancestry (formerly Relative Genetics) (http://dna.ancestry.com/)
- Family Tree DNA (http://www.familytreedna.com/)

Project management facilities were previously offered by DNA Heritage; the company was acquired by Family Tree DNA in April 2011. DNA Heritage results can be transferred free of charge to the Family Tree DNA database. For further information see the DNA Heritage FAQs at http://www.familytreedna.com/faq/answers/default.aspx?faqid=40.

Guild members who are interested in setting up a DNA project as part of their one-name study can email the Guild's DNA Advisor, Susan Meates, at DNA@one-name.org to request advice and assistance. Susan can help with the project set-up and the selection of a testing company. She will also help with negotiations if the member's surname is already included in an existing project. Family Tree DNA have established a priority email address for the benefit of Guild members at Guild@familytreedna.com.

There are a variety of factors to consider when choosing a testing company, such as the project management facilities provided, the range of tests offered, the size of the company's database, and the facility to store samples.

The International Society of Genetic Genealogists (ISOGG) have charts on their web site comparing the Y-DNA and mtDNA tests provided by the most popular genetic genealogy companies:

ISOGG Y-DNA comparison chart: http://www.isogg.org/ydnachart.htm
ISOGG mtDNA comparison chart: http://www.isogg.org/mtdnachart.htm
ISOGG Project Management features: http://www.isogg.org/features.htm

The comparison chart http://www.familytreedna.com/competitive-chart.aspx on the Family Tree DNA website, might also be of interest.

2.5.2 Frequently asked DNA questions

Q: Is there more than one kind of DNA test for genealogy purposes?

A: Yes — for males, Y-chromosome DNA tests examine markers on the Y-chromosome which are handed down virtually intact from father to son across many generations, because a mother has no Y-chromosomes to mix with the father's. For females, mitochondrial DNA (mtDNA) is inherited in a manner similar to Y-DNA in males. However, mtDNA is not associated with particular surnames. Only males can supply a sample for Y-DNA investigation of paternal ancestry, but males or females can supply a sample for mtDNA investigation of maternal ancestry.

Q: What kind of test should be used for a one-name study?

A: In a society where surnames are inherited from the father, the Y-DNA test is the one to use for general lineage purposes.

Q: What do I say to a correspondent whose grandmother (or other female ancestor) was born with "my" surname, who wants to explore their roots in that surname using my study's DNA project?

A: Your correspondent's grandmother (or whoever) probably had brothers or uncles who had your study name. He/she should find one of those brothers/uncles (or a male-line descendant thereof) and persuade him to join your project.

Q: Can an ancestor's hair be tested?

A: Maybe, but it's not easy. A lock of hair cut off with scissors doesn't include any hair roots and therefore has no nuclear DNA (in particular, no Y-DNA), only mtDNA. A complete hair found in a comb or brush might work if it has been kept in a cool, dry place. A tooth might also work, though old shed deciduous teeth (commonly called milk or baby teeth) may not retain the dentine required for a DNA analysis. Even an envelope or stamp that was licked by a known ancestor might have traces of DNA. However, extraction from such sources is a very specialised job, and most testing laboratories don't do that sort of thing. One case that has been examined is hair reputed to come from Sir Isaac Newton, which proved to come from several different people.

Q: What about exhumation?

A: Theoretically possible, though permission to exhume may be difficult to obtain, the DNA tends to break down very quickly if the body has been embalmed and then buried in soil, there may be difficulty identifying the correct grave, and again most testing laboratories do not do that type of test.

Q: Does it hurt?

A: No. The test does not require blood, only a sample of loose cells collected from inside the mouth using a pair of swabs. A kit is mailed to the person being tested, he does the swab himself, and the sample is sent to the laboratory by mail.

Q: Is this anything like paternity testing?

A: They both use DNA but are otherwise very different. For one thing, paternity tests must work for both males and females, but your project's Y-DNA testing will work only for males. Also, Y-DNA testing cannot pick out a person's father from among a collection of his same-surname male relatives.

Q: Is this anything like the tests used for identifying criminals?

A: No, those are generally the same as paternity tests.

Q: Is this anything like the screening tests used by insurance companies?

A: No. The markers tested for genealogy do not detect diseases.

Q: What can people learn from this testing?

A: In simple terms, it will determine (very approximately) how closely a person is related to other people who take the test.

Q: Doesn't this testing reveal mutations? Aren't mutations bad?

A: The markers examined have no genetic function, and therefore mutations in them are harmless. In fact, the mutations are useful for genealogical purposes, since they distinguish one family from another.

2.5.3 Publicising your DNA project

Guild publicity

If you have not already done so you should compile a profile page so that your study is publicised on the Guild's own website. Instructions for setting up a profile page can be found in the Members' Room. If you already have a profile page, note that there is a section on your profile page where you can write about your DNA project.

Ensure that your project is included in the list of Guild DNA websites in the Members' Room. To add your project to the list fill out the URL of your DNA website on the "Check your study details" form in the Members' Room. Note that the online register supports the submission of a DNA website in addition to an ONS website for each registered surname.

Mailing lists

Rootsweb host a variety of surname and geographical mailing lists. Choose your wording carefully and do not cross-post the same message to multiple lists. It is wise to get a feel for a mailing list first before posting a message.

Message boards

Post an announcement about your project on the appropriate surname message boards at Rootsweb and Genforum.

In addition there is a dedicated Rootsweb message board for the announcement of new DNA projects

Rootschat have a dedicated one-name studies board which also includes a special section for GOONS members.

Websites

Members of the International Society of Genetic Genealogy can post an announcement about their project on the society's website.

Cyndi's List has a special section for DNA surname projects.

If you belong to the social networking site Facebook you can set up a surname group where you can add a link to your DNA project.

Other sites where you can add links include:

- Linkpendium (http://www.linkpendium.com)
- My Cinnamon Toast listing of DNA studies (http://www.mycinnamontoast.com/perl/results.cgi?region=0&type=31&sort=n)
- Rootsweb surname list (http://rsl.rootsweb.ancestry.com/
- Surname finder (http://www.surnamefinder.com/)

Family History Societies

If you belong to a family history society it might be possible to publish an announcement about your DNA project in the society's journal. Journal editors might even welcome an article about your DNA project or a short feature on a success story.

2.5.4 Case study: The Dorling DNA project

My experience of setting up a surname project with DNA Heritage by Karen Hemmingham

I chose DNA Heritage because they were offering the best price for a lot of markers: 43. In February and March 2006 there was a special offer of £75 for 43 markers but it is usually around £95, though it varies with the exchange rate.

It was extremely quick and easy to set up the project by simply filling in details on the appropriate web page. I could also leave information on the site for others to view, e.g. website address, aims of the surname project. Others can search the site to see if a surname is part of a project and email you (if you've chosen to have your email address available) or leave a message in the message box on your project page.

I became the administrator and was given a web address to give to others so they could join the project (you can have co-administrators). I can also input people's details to enrol them, which I have done for someone who doesn't have a computer and another who wanted to leave all the organisation to me. As administrator, I can view everyone's details and results. Once someone has signed up I can see if the test kit has been sent out, if it has been received back, if the results are back, and if the full report has been sent out to the person tested. No payment is required until the test sample has been received by the company and then an invoice is sent by email to both myself and the person whose sample it is. Payment online is easy with credit or debit card. I have found the whole process very straightforward and have had no problems other than persuading people to join the project!

An important point is that you need two distant relatives from a branch in order to confirm the DNA sequence for that branch.

Main aims of the Dorling Surname Project:

- To discover the genetic sequence that identifies the main branches of the Dorling surname, namely, the Bacton, Bury St Edmunds, West Stow, Epsom, Barton Mills, Dennington, Easton, Herringswell, and Framsden branches.
- To help confirm the findings of genealogical research into the Dorling family trees and suggest possible avenues of future research.
- To discover whether any of the main branches are related to each other via a common ancestor and if so to estimate how many generations back to the common ancestor.
- To discover how individuals and other smaller branches of Dorlings fit into the overall Dorling history, either as distinct branches or as part of other Dorling branches.
- To provide the potential means of identifying the male ancestry of a branch originating from a female Dorling.
- To investigate the deeper ancestral roots of the Dorling families.

Progressing the project

Getting people to join up is the hardest part. DNA Heritage provide a letter which you can use and add to if you want. For our project I wrote personal emails or letters and provided extra information on DNA testing for people to read if they wanted. I also put information on my website and gave links to the tutorials on the DNA Heritage website. Three people initially joined the project and later on I ended up offering to pay in an attempt to get more people and have subsequently shared the cost with some and paid completely for others. As of November 2006 we have nine results for five of the main Dorling branches and another result from one of these branch due in November 2006. The DNA results are exciting because they tell us something we don't yet know from standard research about the relationships between the different branches, as well as verifying traditional research.

Results

The results are a series of numbers, one for each marker. A match of 40+ out of 43 suggests a recent common ancestor, recent meaning within the era of surnames. You are also told which DNA haplogroup they probably fit into. Once you have several results DNA Heritage do some interpretation for you – I haven't got enough results yet.

My results to date:

The two Bury St Edmunds (BSE) descendant tests show identical results and provide a reference for other BSE Dorlings who are should have the same DNA signature. It shows that their deep ancestry is from a haplogroup common in Europe – R1b.

The two West Stow results are one marker different to each other, and a 42/43 and 41/43 match with BSE. So it seems the West Stow Dorlings are related to the BSE ones, sharing a common ancestor. However, one of the West Stow descendants appears to have a recent mutation in one of the DNA marker numbers thus making two markers different from the BSE DNA. I have found it is easier to describe this relationship in a tree, which I can email to anyone interested.

Finding the common ancestor of the BSE and West Stow branch is now one of the major aims of my one-name study.

The two Bacton results match each other and are very unusual results, having six values for marker DYS 464 instead of the usual four. The Bacton results are part of the J2 haplogroup which is very uncommon in Europe – about 1% of the UK population have this DNA group.

I also have one result for the Nacton-Easton branch which is R1b and does not match any of the other Dorling DNA results. We are now awaiting the results of a 2nd Nacton-Easton descendant. The result for the Dennington-Epsom branch does not match any other branches. The result for the Barton Mills branch again matches none of the other Dorling branches and has been identified as haplotype I1bI which is rare in the UK and common in Sardinia! Having different haplogroups means there is no chance of being related other than perhaps in very ancient times, e.g the stone age!

I now need to find a distant relative within the Dennington, Barton Mills and Nacton-Easton branches to be tested so we can confirm that the results truly represent that branch and are not the result of a more recent non-paternity or adoption event. I also need to find participants for the branches so far untested.

I have put my results on my website so if anyone wants to see what they look like they can link to my DNA page by clicking on DNA in the navigation bar at the top of my home page: http://dorling-ancestry.mysite.wanadoo-members.co.uk/.

3. Synthesis

Synthesis is about using the results of your analysis to draw conclusions about your name and create 'added value'.

Important areas for synthesis are drawing conclusions on:

- The meaning of the surname
- The geographical origin of the surname – for which maps help present results
- How and where name variants arose
- The main patterns of distribution change, including emigration and immigration

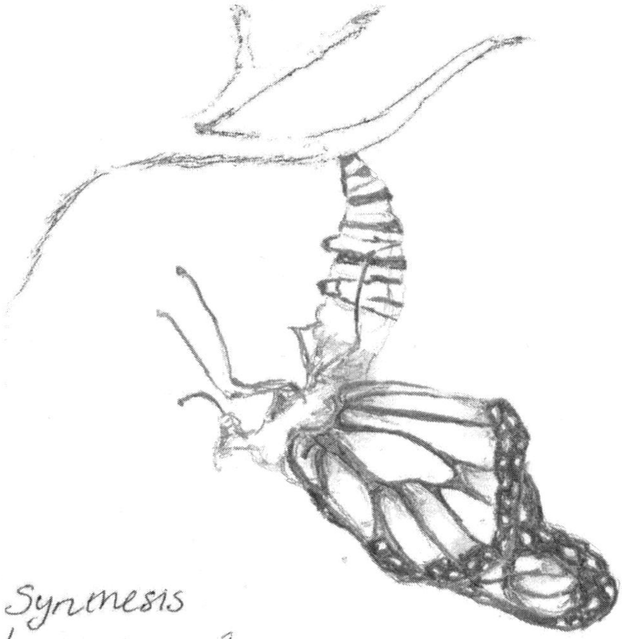

However, many other conclusions can be drawn, such as longevity, morbidity, infant mortality, number of pregnancies, illegitimacy rates, social conditions, impact of extended families, and distance between places of birth and marriage. Many social scientists could be interested in such material.

Most one-name researchers do not propose to "complete" their studies in the sense of exhaustively collecting every scrap of information in the world; they are regularly evaluating progress to see if the study is mature enough to yield reliable conclusions about the name and its users.

3.1 Meaning of the surname

Surnames are generally formed from the following types:

- Patronymic
  - Jones, Richardson, Williams, Bowen, Pritchard, Hobson, Perkins, Eriksdottir
- Matronymic
  - Margetson, Dyson, Megson
- Genitive
  - Squires, Manners
- Diminutive
  - Alcock, Watkin, Bartlett
- Locative (topographical)
  - Green, Hill, Langridge, Townsend
- Locative (toponymic)
  - Stepney, Helmsley, Beckham
- Occupational
  - Baker, Fletcher, Thatcher, Pargeter, Smith
  -

- Postholder
    - Hayward, Bailey
- Nicknames/Physical Appearance
    - Redhead, Fox, Longfellow, Cruikshank, Toogood

If your study name has multiple origins, it may also have multiple meanings.

For a more extended discussion of the different types of surnames and their different distributions in the Anglophone world see the papers from a conference on *Surnames as a quantitative resource: the geography of British and Anglophone Surnames* (26th-27th April, 2004). These are available at http://www.casa.ucl.ac.uk/surnames/papers.htm.

The origin of Irish surnames is described in three excellent articles:

- *A note on the emergence of Irish surnames*, Francis Byrne in *Irish Kings and High Kings*, 2001 edition, pp xxxi-xlvii
- *The formation of Gaelic surnames in Ireland: choosing the eponym*, D. O Murchadha in *Nomina* 22 (1999) pp 25-44
- *Aspects of an early Irish surname: Ua Canannáin*, T. Ó Canann in *Studia Hibernica*, 27 (1993), pp 113-44

An excellent academic study of the origins of Scottish surnames is Matthew Hammond's 2005 Ph.D. on early Scottish prosopography (http://theses.gla.ac.uk/1076/)

Philip Dance's bibliography (http://homepages.newnet.co.uk/dance/webpjd/intro/britbib.htm) of works relating to names includes many surname dictionaries, as does the Thesaurus of British Surnames (ToBS) bibliography (http://www.tobs.org.uk/bib/index.html).

3.1.2 Useful websites

Great Britain

- Institute for Name Studies: http://www.nottingham.ac.uk/english/ins
- National Trust names website: http://www.nationaltrustnames.org.uk/
- Behind the name: the etymology and history of surnames: http://surnames.behindthename.com/
- The relevance of surnames in genealogy — A useful leaflet from the Society of Genealogists: http://www.sog.org.uk/leaflets/leaflets.shtml
- Modern British Surnames: a Resource Guide: http://www.modbritnames.co.uk
- Surnames of England and Wales, the ONS list: http://www.taliesin-arlein.net/names/search.php
- The Internet Surname Database: http://www.surnamedb.com
- Occupational surnames: http://www.namenerds.com/uucn/listofweek/jobnames.html

Ireland

- Old Irish-Gaelic Surnames: http://www.rootsweb.ancestry.com/~irlkik/ihm/irenames.htm

USA

- American Name Society: http://www.wtsn.binghamton.edu/ans
- US surname distribution: http://hamrick.com/names

3.2 Origin of the surname

The strict origin of a surname is where either:

- A person adopted a second name to his forename and this became hereditary through his descendants; or
- A person adopted his father's 'byname' and it became hereditary. Most bynames were originally locative or occupational suffixes specific to that individual.

For an occupational name, like Smith or Walker, there will not be a single origin. However, many topographical names or even those based on nicknames can have a single origin despite initial assumptions. It is easy to see how nicknames and names suggesting physical characteristics became bynames, but is less easy to see why some less flattering ones were adopted as hereditary surnames. Perhaps, like bynames, some surnames were 'imposed'. In more recent times, immigrants to the USA were encouraged to adopt anglicised versions of their original name, so starting another 'origin' for the name.

Of course, surnames can also pass through a female in the case of an illegitimate child or be given to adopted children.

You may never be able to find this strict origin, but it is always useful to collect examples of the very earliest references to the name you can find, e.g. Lay Subsidies, Poll Tax records etc. However, modern research suggests that many of the early references may give a false picture of the surname origin. Firstly, the names found may still be 'bynames' and not then hereditary. Secondly, the male descendants of that person may have not survived and the modern holders of the name may have a separate origin. Mapping the earliest names with a proven descent to modern times may give a different picture.

3.3 Lineage reconstruction

Lineage reconstruction by one-namers often follows the common method of family historians and genealogists: using birth/baptism, marriage and household census records to link parents to children. One-namers may have the advantage over genealogists of being able to eliminate possible matches or confirm matches because they are confident that they know all of the people living in a certain district in a certain period bearing the surname.

Working with multiple families which are not related to one another, or numerous descendants of a single family, requires some method of labelling the families, or lineages, in order to keep track of them. For ideas on how to do this, see *1.6.1: Systems of naming*, above.

While genealogy demands nothing less than a **precise lineage**, one-name researchers often count themselves lucky if they can establish an **approximate lineage**. The data collection may only yield up fragmentary lineages, of two or three generations at a stretch, and the researcher cannot link these short chains with certainty into a longer lineage. Some one-name studies may lack substantial parent-child data altogether.

In these cases, it may be useful to publish a tabulation of all the named individuals, grouped by the districts in which they lived and worked and the historical periods when they were economically active (usually denoted by the Latin verb *floruit*). These groupings by the researcher can be arranged in nodes at 25- or 33-year intervals from one another. If the one-name study is not too large, it is likely that each of these nodes marks an extended contemporary family of siblings and cousins.

Data about class, professions, educational achievement, landholdings and wealth can also be useful in teasing out these approximate lineages, since it is likeliest that children imitated their parents' methods, repeated their vocations and conserved their wealth, and less likely that two families would have swapped their places on the social ladder.

Approximate lineages, which are for example common in pre-19th-century Irish family history, can be a valuable contribution to micro-history.

3.4 Illegitimacy rates

The historical rate of illegitimacy is a long-debated topic among local historians, specifically how and why it has changed.

The underlying rate is of special interest to admins of surname-based DNA projects: a high rate would likely stimulate the formation of many 'new' trees with distinct DNA patterns within the ONS, while a low rate would mean that few such trees were created (and the surname would tend to look more as though it has a single genetic origin).

The Office for National Statistics (http://www.statistics.gov.uk) have statistics on their website on the number of births within and outside marriage in England and Wales. It is likely however that there will be considerable differences in the rates seen within individual studies. The General Register Office for Scotland (http://www.gro-scotland.gov.uk/statistics/) have birth figures grouped by marital status of parents.

Earlier illegitimacy rates were estimated in Peter Laslett and Karla Oosterveen's article "*Long-Term Trends in Bastardy in England: A Study of the Illegitimacy Figures in the Parish Registers and in the Reports of the Registrar General, 1561-1960*" (*Population Studies* vol.27 pp.255-286, 1973). From a sample of 24 parishes they reconstructed rates varying between 0.5 and 6.3% of baptised children as bastards in each decade between 1581 and 1810. There are problems reconstructing the rate in the period 1810-1843, but after this the GRO data can be used. This study considered those children noted as bastards or where only the mother's name was given in the baptism register as illegitimate. For some of these the parents may subsequently have married, thus legitimating the child, and of course those children born to married women but not fathered by their husband are not detected. They also found regional differences in illegitimacy rates.

The raw data below is taken from birth registrations at the General Register Office in the Pomeroy ONS. To date the study has found:

Period	*Reg's*	*#*	*Rate*	*GRO average*
1837-1899	2,279	28	1.2%	5.5% (1845-1899)
1900-1945	1,667	46	2.8%	4.6%
1946-2005	2,152	239	11.1%	16.3%

The figures prior to 1912 are underestimates as the status of a significant number of children who were born and died between census periods have not yet been checked.

The figures between 1901-1912 may be slightly underestimated as around 20 births are not yet allocated to family trees, some of which may turn out to be illegitimacies.

The figures may be slightly overstated as there were 8 'inter-ONS' marriages during the period; children from these unions would appear in the above statistics.

No figures are given of children who appear in censuses as Pomeroys but for whom no birth record has been found; these may well be children brought into the surname through the (re)marriage of their mother.

Note that these figures above represent registrations (or certificates) where the mother's maiden name is one of the three names in the Pomeroy ONS. These conflate traditional illegitimacies (where no father's name appears) and post-war instances where the father's name is present but the parents are or appear to be unmarried. From the point of view of a DNA study the effect is identical: male Pomeroy DNA is not passed on to the surname-bearing children and thus male line descendants will carry a different Y-chromosome DNA signature.

The traditional linkage between the father's surname and the child's surname is rapidly breaking down. In 2005, 34% of Pomeroy ONS-covered birth registrations cited a mother's name within the ONS: 10 of these were boys (out of 24 male child registrations).

3.5 Evaluating progress

While some one-namers nurse the objective of "completing" their study, in the sense of collecting all the biographical data that exists, most people doing a one-name study are conserving their research energies while maximizing their knowledge about the community of people sharing a single surname.

Like other scientific methods, one-naming can be described as a set of labour-saving procedures and analytical methods to efficiently achieve a large degree of knowledge. The aim of a ONS is not the collection of data as such: collection is a means to an end. The aim of a ONS is to ascertain, amongst other things:

- Origin of the name or early references
- The name's meaning (is it patronymic, topographical, toponymic, occupational, etc?)
- Its relative frequency
- Its distribution in geography and time
- Patterns of immigration and emigration
- Name variants and 'deviants'

When the researcher begins to grasp the answers to these questions, the ONS can be said to have reached maturity.

An ONS does not have to reconstruct families to achieve maturity. If you can (as you often can for the UK), then that is icing on the cake, but some studies will achieve fruition as annotated biographical indexes with only limited lineage information.

To evaluate how much progress you have made towards a mature ONS, a variety of factors have to be considered, including the accessibility of the necessary indexes, the size of the human group you are studying, the representativeness of the data you have found, the spread of sources that you have checked with both positive and negative results, and your skill in interpreting the data.

3.5.1 Accessibility of indexes

One-name research is mainly conducted on countries (a) where feasibility surveys have shown the name exists and (b) where it is practical to get hold of useful "one-name" resources.

The ONS method is supremely productive in Britain, because Britain is the only major industrialised nation in the world with open-access, national indexes of vital data. If your study name occurs mainly in England and Wales, then once you have harvested the GRO data and census data, you can say you have tracked down 95 per cent of people with your study name for most of the 19th and 20th centuries.

In other European nations such as Germany, the one-name method is largely unproductive, because the only open-access national indexes are the IGI and VRI, the telephone directory and the internet. The only conceivable alternative to a one-name study would be to do a global genealogy of all pre-20th-century Germans with a certain, widely distributed surname: you would have to visit dozens of archives and survey thousands of baptismal registers and it would take thousands of hours of work. One-name studies (known in German as *Namensträgerforschung*) are only rarely attempted on German names, and usually only for tightly restricted surnames with unique locations where there is already a strong body of pre-existing research.

If indexes and other secondary material are not available for the geographical area that you pinpoint as the name's homeland in your early research, it may not be possible to bring the ONS to maturity.

3.5.2 Size of the surname community

There has been considerable debate within the Guild about whether a one-name study of an extremely common surname is even possible in the existing sense. The prevalence of the small and medium study size is discussed in several places in the Wiki. A Celtic clan name or an occupational surname which may have been separately adopted by thousands of tradesmen in the 14th century may create such a blur of data that it is impossible to pick out places of origin or patterns of migration. Generally, an ONS of a surname with just one, two or three localities of origin is much easier to bring to maturity.

3.5.3 Size of the sample

Because a ONS trawls through a wide variety of documentary sources, the researcher collects a large number of "stray" persons who cannot initially be connected into the geographical subdivisions or families. With time, many of the persons in a database can be grouped into families and others can at least be identified with geographical groups. Sometimes it will be discovered that people of quite different origins also share the name, for example ethnic German migrants to the United States who acquire an English surname, and these will be recorded but noted as belonging to the out-group. However, a large number of names will remain as strays, even in a mature study.

An analysis of strays can be a useful indicator of the accuracy of the information sample and hence of the maturity of the study. If the locations and historical periods of the strays closely match those of the fully researched groups, it is possible to argue that the sample of intensively researched families or villages is representative of the whole.

It should always be assumed that a fraction of families will not yet have been detected at all by an ONS. But it is generally found that the proportion of stray data to the whole usually far exceeds the proportion of undetected village groups or families to the whole.

3.5.4 Spread

The Guild recommends a short survey of likely countries before you register a surname. This avoids you starting a study of a rare UK name that turns out to be very common, say, in the USA. A quick trawl of the US 1880 census index and the SSDI would be sensible, for example and gives you a good core of US data with which to start.

To achieve maturity, a true one-name study must include some work with the global resources identified by the Guild Wiki, and a report on the worldwide incidence of the name. For sources, see the section *1.2: Sources of Documentary data* above, and the Wiki itself. For example, this could mean a search of the International Genealogical Index, web search engines, contemporary online newspapers, online telephone directories, databases of authors and patent files.

If you search the global indexes, and never find your name outside the areas being researched with national indexes, it is possible to argue that the study has accurately detected the surname's area of origin.

3.5.5 Skill

While it might seem immodest to advertise the fact about your own study, your skills are a main factor in bringing a study to rapid maturity. The one-name method allows us to use the limited information found in indexes to make an educated assessment about the global presence of a name without examining every documentary source.

The analytical skill of the researcher in picking out patterns can be enhanced by careful record-keeping, by genealogical research into similar names from the same region, and by developing a knowledge of the region's social and political history. Experience is vital to judge which indexes can be relied on.

For example, entries in the International Genealogical Index that are derived from controlled extraction programmes carry a far greater weight for the one-namer than IGI data derived from LDS members' own genealogies. An awareness of whether indexes were compiled by optical character recognition, offshore transcription or by indexers with local knowledge is central in deciding whether one is dealing with a variant spelling or a mere copying mistake.

4. Publicising your study

The one-namer will need to make his study known, in order to attract the attention of potential contributors of information. Various forms of advertising are recommended.

Publicising your Study
Madeleine Jacob age 11

Don't be disappointed if you don't get many enquiries, even after you've joined the Guild. By their very nature, rare names are not going to be of widespread interest.

4.1 Magazines and Journals

Many one-namers find it useful to have a recurring advertisement in one or more of the various Family History magazines. For instance, Family Tree Magazine runs a specific one-name column where a one-name "small-ad" can be placed for a reasonable fee. (At one time the Genealogical Research Directory was the accepted place for such small-ads, but this is now defunct.)

- Family Tree Magazine (http://www.family-tree.co.uk) (small ads in one-name column)
- Other magazines
- Family history society journals

Of course, it need hardly be said that inclusion in the Guild's annual Register is a significant contribution to publicising a one-name study.

4.2 Websites

4.2.1 Your own website

One-name study websites are likely to be the most effective way to promulgate studies. If you are not confident enough to create one, the Guild's profile facility will help you get online with a simple advertising page. However, since a website is an effective way to publish your study's results as well as furthering the study by getting it known, it may be worth acquiring website skills, in which case you would benefit from the advice given below under *6.1: One-name study websites*.

You will also want to make sure your website features high up in the results from search engines such as Google. See below, *4.2.5: Improving your search engine rankings*, for advice on this.

4.2.2 The Guild Profile

As well as the publicity provided through the Guild's Register and perhaps your own website, don't neglect to set up your Guild Profile. This has proved for many members to be an extremely effective way to drive enquiries to their one-name study. The process of setting up a profile is very simple, takes only a few minutes, and is built around a standard template common to all profiles.

4.2.3 Registering and advertising on other websites

- Cyndi's List (http://www.cyndislist.com/)
- Rootsweb mailing lists (http://lists.rootsweb.ancestry.com)
- Rootsweb surname list (http://rsl.rootsweb.ancestry.com)
- Facebook (http://www.facebook.com). Many Guild members have now set up surname groups on Facebook – see *4.3: Social Networking* below
- MyHeritage (http://www.myheritage.com)
- Surname pages on Geni.com (http://www.geni.com/surnames)
- Genuki (http://www.genuki.org.uk/)
- GenesReunited (http://www.genesreunited.com/)
- Lost Cousins (http://www.lostcousins.com)
- British-Genealogy.com (http://www.british-genealogy.com/) (and overseas equivalents)
- Relevant county surname lists (http://www.genuki.org.uk/indexes/SurnamesLists.html)
- Family History Societies' Members' Interests lists
- The Society of Genealogists (http://www.sog.org.uk/)
- Roots Chat (http://www.rootschat.com) have a dedicated One Name Interests Common Room at http://www.rootschat.com/forum/index.php/board,151.0.html which has a special section for Guild members. There is also a Surname Interests Board at http://surname.rootschat.com.

4.2.4 Wikipedia surname page

Remember that Wikipedia is an encyclopaedia first and foremost. It is not an opportunity to publicise your project, and if the Wikipedia admins suspect you of publishing promotional material they will remove it very quickly.

Wikipedia has its own manual of style, and a preferred order in which information is to be presented in its articles. This manual of style can be viewed at http://en.wikipedia.org/wiki/Wikipedia:Manual_of_style.

There is a disclaimer at the bottom of every edit window regarding ownership of the content, copyright, licensing and terms of use. It is helpful to be familiar with these but, in a nutshell, once you press the "save" button you agree that any content you have uploaded is the property of the Wikimedia Foundation headquartered in Florida, United States, and as such is subject to Florida state copyright law, and released under the GFDL Creative Commons Attribution/Share-Alike License.

That means that you cease to "own" the information after you have saved it, and other users are within their rights to come along and edit it, change it or remove it altogether.

You can lessen the degree to which this happens by making sure the content you add is referenced using reliable sources that demonstrate its notability. Policies on each of these concepts in Wikipedia can be found in the Wikipedia articles on *Citing sources, Identifying reliable sources*, and *Notability*:

- http://en.wikipedia.org/wiki/Wikipedia:Citing_sources
- http://en.wikipedia.org/wiki/Wikipedia:Identifying_reliable_sources
- http://en.wikipedia.org/wiki/Wikipedia:Notability

Please don't copy and paste information from any source into Wikipedia: they have bots that spot this kind of thing and remove it almost instantaneously. Furthermore "original research" is frowned upon: if you can't prove using reliable information that is accessible by others that what you are saying is true then, even if it is true, it may still be removed from the project.

In terms of our projects, the Wikipedia requirement for online citation can be a URL link to our own webpage, or Guild profile, but better still would be a link to an online report describing the project's status and results. It would be even better if that report were in a third-party publication.

Having said all that, good articles do exist on surnames at the project. You can sign up and begin editing immediately. But to get the most out of the experience it's worth familiarising yourself with the above first.

4.2.5 Improving your search engine rankings

There are two main strategies: generate more good links to your site, and make your homepage more informative.

Links can be generated through a signature line on emails and by submitting your site to lists of genealogy links.

The best signatures and short entries on lists of links have relevant words close to a functioning link to your site which uses the full URL, e.g.,

    http://www.bloggs.com/

rather than just the domain name, e.g.,

    www.bloggs.com

Many sites which archive email messages (including Rootsweb) will automatically make something beginning "http://" into a link, but may not recognise the domain name on its own as a link. If you are competing for rankings with someone or something in popular culture then adding the words 'genealogy' and/or 'family history' might help you to get to the top of the rankings for those making more specific searches. This would probably be quite a good signature line:

> For the family history and genealogy of Blog, Blogg and Bloggs,
> visit http://www.bloggs.com/

Including major variants helps put you at the top of Google rankings for them as well.

4.2.5.1 Some hints on improving Google rankings

- Go to Cyndi's list (http://www.cyndislist.com/surn-gen.htm) and work your way through all the surname websites. Lots of them have the facility for you to tell them about your website and/or profile page. Some, like Linkpendium, seem to pick up the names automatically, whereas others will include a link only if you tell them that you exist.

- Post messages on the Rootsweb (http://boards.ancestry.com/) and Genealogy.com (http://genforum.genealogy.com/) message boards for your study name providing links to your website and/or profile page. If there aren't any message boards for your study name then create them. Include the link in a signature line every time you post.

- Ask the admin for the relevant page of the County look-up exchange (if there is one – http://aztecrose.tripod.com/LookupExchange.htm) to include a link to your website and/or profile page.

- Make sure you include the URL of your web page and/or profile page in the signature line of your postings to all your Rootsweb mailing lists. Most email clients have the facility to create a customised signature which can simply be pasted at the end of your emails to avoid having to re-type all the information afresh.

- Inform the relevant Rootsweb surname mailing lists (http://lists.rootsweb.com) about your website and/or profile page.

- It is not just the quantity of links which is important but the *quality* of those links. Try and get your website and/or profile page linked from high-traffic websites such as Wikipedia (http://en.wikipedia.org/wiki) or Genuki (http://www.genuki.org.uk). Wikipedia has a collection of surname pages and it is possible to include an external link to your website or profile page at the bottom of the relevant page. If a page does not exist for your study name you can create one, though you will have to create a Wikipedia user account to do so. It is sometimes possible to include links to your website or profile page from the appropriate parish page on Genuki.

- If you have specialist information on your website or profile page (for instance, material about the Army, Navy, or RAF), arrange for links to be included on the appropriate specialist websites, mailing lists and message boards. The Medieval Genealogy Website has a Families page and the webmaster is happy to include links to one-name studies of medieval families.

- Take a careful look at the content of your web page and/or profile page and make sure you use the relevant key words which will help people to find you. Place names are particularly important, so include as many as possible in the "distribution" section of your profile page.

- For the technically minded, Academic Genealogy have some very helpful links on http://www.academic-genealogy.com/genealogywebmasters.htm. The Wikipedia page on Search engine optimisation is also particularly informative.

- Be patient. It takes several months for all the above measures to have any effect on your Google rankings.

- Don't despair if Google mysteriously drop you from their rankings. It seems to happen every few months or so but it is only a temporary measure and normally only lasts a couple of days.

- Cheer yourself up by checking your rankings with some other search engines such as Yahoo, Lycos, AltaVista and MSN. They take longer to list your website but often seem to give higher rankings than Google, and don't mysteriously drop you for a few days at a time for no reason.

4.3 Social Networking (Facebook, etc.)

The new social networking websites such as Facebook have proved extremely fruitful for making contacts in your ONS.

4.3.1 Facebook for one-name studies

Facebook is now one of the most popular websites in the world with an astonishing 800 million active users worldwide (http://www.facebook.com/press/info.php?statistics). The Social Bakers website has statistics on Facebook penetration on a country-by-country basis at http://www.socialbakers.com/facebook-statistics/.

In many countries, including the US and the UK, around half of the population have a Facebook account. You will, therefore, find more people with your study name on Facebook than on any other website in the world. In an age when many people choose to opt out of the public electoral register, have an ex-directory telephone number or no landline whatsoever, Facebook can often be the easiest way of establishing contact with other researchers.

Facebook is also an excellent way of keeping in touch with your existing contact network. It is often easier to contact people via Facebook rather than by email, and it is also very handy when people have problems with their email system. A growing number of genealogists are using Facebook and most genealogy organisations now have a presence on Facebook.

A Facebook account can be set up free of charge. You will need to register with your usual email address so that you can receive notifications.

In order to get an idea of how Facebook works it is suggested that in the first instance you join the Guild's Facebook group at http://www.facebook.com/group.php?gid=4250564090. This is a closed group which is restricted to Guild members only. The group works in a very similar way to a mailing list and you can arrange to be notified by email whenever someone posts to the group. The notifications can be adjusted as required using the notifications tab in the top right-hand corner of the group page.

It is also worth "liking" the Guild's Facebook fan page, which can be found at http://www.facebook.com/guildonename. This is a public page, and is open to both members and non-members. As well as keeping Guild members notified of interesting news stories and new websites, the page also serves as a promotional tool for the Guild. Any posts from the Guild will appear in your newsfeed – the page that you see when you log into Facebook. To see if there are any other genealogy pages of interest click on the Guild's list of "likes".

4.3.2 Promoting your one-name study on Facebook

Many Guild members are using Facebook as a means to promote their one-name study. You can choose to set up either a group or a page. The Facebook FAQ explains the differences between pages and groups and provides links to get you started: http://www.facebook.com/help/?faq=155275634539412.

The ***groups*** are more like mailing lists. If someone posts a message in the group everyone receives an email notification unless they've opted out. You effectively act as a list administrator. You can leave all the group members to chat to each other and only step in if you have anything to add to the conversation. Group members can also upload photos which can be shared with all group members.

The ***fan pages*** are intended more for businesses and organisations and are a one-way broadcast. Everything you post is seen by your fans, so long as they check their Facebook page regularly and see the news feeds. Not everyone checks their Facebook page on a regular basis so many of your posts will not necessarily be seen by everyone. Fans can comment on posts, but they can't interact with each other in the same way that they can with the groups. If someone posts something on your page wall, for instance, only the admins get a notification. With a fan page it's therefore up to you to do all the work and to publish posts on a regular basis.

For most one-namers a group is probably the best option. Groups can be open or closed. Open groups have all their posts visible to the general public and will appear in search engine results. Closed groups are restricted to members and the posts cannot be seen in public.

You should advertise your new Facebook group on your profile page and/or your website and include the relevant link. If you are Facebook "friends" with other people researching your name you can add them to the group. It's a good idea to get the group started by uploading a few photos of your own, but be careful only to use out-of-copyright photos and do not post any photos of living people without their permission. You can also use the Facebook messaging system to send out invites to people with your study name. Make sure you do not send out too many invites at once as you will be suspected of spamming.

Some examples of Guild surname group can be seen here:

- Cruse – http://www.facebook.com/groups/cruse/
- Kirkman – http://www.facebook.com/groups/359394404081/
- Swinfield – http://www.facebook.com/groups/321619050985/

And an example of a Guild surname fan page:

- Owston – http://www.facebook.com/owstonouston

4.3.3 Collecting genealogy information on Facebook

Facebook can also be used to extract genealogy information for your one-name study. If you are "friends" with people with your study name you will have access to their profiles and any details they have published about themselves and their family. Sometimes they will share news of family births, weddings and deaths in their status updates. Public profile pages can also be mined for genealogical information. Bear in mind that Facebook does not make any checks on the accuracy of user-submitted data, and people will often use an incorrect birth date or show the wrong country as their place of residence.

Some useful links to websites and details of books about Facebook are available in the Guild Wiki.

4.4 New.familysearch.org

Another new way to publicise the existence of your study is via the new LDS website facility, "new.familysearch.org", (http://new.familysearch.org) which the LDS are (hopefully) about to roll out to the general public. Despite the confusing name, this is totally separate from the "new" FamilySearch data website available at familysearch.org and originally introduced as http://pilot.familysearch.org.

The new.familysearch.org website has a very different purpose from the record collections at familysearch.org. In effect it is a huge pedigree chart, maintained by LDS members and staff. It is a totally new website, piloted by the LDS Church and currently open only to LDS members and those non-members receiving invitations, which has links to other sources of information on the surnames entered for searching. One such link to additional information is to the Guild resources: if the user enters a surname which is registered with the Guild, then he is offered a "Guild" link and can click on it to go to the Guild register search results for that name.

It is designed to work in combination with SharingTime, a web facility developed in conjunction with FamilySearch. Users need to install a SharingTime plug-in to their browser, and will need accounts on both FamilySearch and SharingTime.

Disappointingly, this new website with its new functionality is not yet (at the time of writing) available to the general public. Guild members, however, are among those invited to preview the facility, and details of how Guild members can get started are in the Members Room as one of the Articles of Interest under the "Information" tab.

But the usefulness of this website as a method of publicising a surname study will be severely limited until it is made generally available to the public.

4.5 Mailshots

Writing letters or emails to bearers of the surname can be a productive way to gain new contacts and new information. The best guide to this process is Peter Amsden's booklet *Making Contact With Relatives* published by FFHS in 1999; this is no longer available, but Peter has made a pdf version available to Guild members, and this can be downloaded from the Members Room. The discussion below draws on advice given on the Guild Forum rather than repeating the booklet.

There are several issues to consider.

4.5.1 Garnering addresses

The best sources vary by country.

- **Telephone directories** are frequently good sources, but in some countries and places (e.g. London) there are very high proportions of ex-directory subscribers.
- **UK electoral roll** has been found by some to be better than the 'phone directory, but use a version from 2004 or before, as since then over 70% of the voters have taken the "ex-roll" option. Although some people will have moved, it will still give better coverage than the 2007/8 roll. Also, the ones who have moved tend to be less likely to reply.
- **email addresses**, found on the internet, through Google, Facebook, etc., are often a more likely route to a response from younger people.

4.5.2 Who to contact

- Don't try to contact everyone. Even for small studies with a few hundred individuals, sending SAEs to the whole lot would be expensive.
- Consider what do you already know about these people? From your existing database, you may already know who many of them are and whether they occupy pivotal points in various trees of the name.
- Avoid duplication and expense by choosing initially one member of a known subtree or geographical group. If they don't reply, you can try another member of the group a few months later. If you contact them all at once, you can spend money only to end up repeatedly getting the same information.
- If your aim is to link all living bearers of the name into trees, then exclude those people whose ancestry you already know.

4.5.3 Maximising response rate

- Target older people first rather than younger people, who are less likely to be interested in Family History. If you don't know their ages, leave out the Waynes and Tracys and other "young" names, and contact the Gladyses, Stanleys and Hildas. If they are in residential care, they might take a while to reply, but might get younger members of the family involved.
- Don't waste time writing to divorcees who have kicked their ex into touch! On the other hand, sometimes it may not be easy to tell a divorcee from a recent widow who may be interested.
- Make it very clear that you are not seeking any money. One member was advised by an American friend that Americans tend to discard any letters that might want money; this is probably true around the world.

4.5.4 The content of the letter

- Older people might benefit from a different wording, perhaps use a more formal approach: Dear Mrs Bloggs, rather than Dear Ada.
- Keep it short; people don't want long letters from strangers.
- Introduce yourself and your relationship to the name.
- Explain how the mailshot relates to the aims of your one-name study.
- Give contact details (including email address).
- Enclose a stamped, addressed envelope or IRCs for any replies.
- Mention spelling variants from the outset. You can use the approach that you are a researcher trying to establish how the various spellings are linked.

- Consider including some brief generic information that you think they might be interested in, e.g. if your research has already indicated a common ancestor for the surname at an approximate date and location.
- It is probably best not to mention DNA in an initial contact, as without a detailed explanation many people will be frightened of giving away genetic information.
- Closing with something like “If family history is of no interest to you, please accept my apologies for bothering you” – that sometimes shames them into replying!
- Information to request:
    - A form can help elicit the information you are interested in. Peter Amsden’s book includes a sample form.
    - Invite them to draw a family tree on any form they return.
    - Ask whether or not they wish to be kept informed of the progress of the ONS (most will say yes if put that way).
    - If you produce a newsletter, include a recent edition. Alternatively consider making a little leaflet to go with the letter.

4.5.5 Repeat mailshots

Guild members who have tried mailshots have typically had a 25% success rate (a range of 15-33% for any one mailshot). One member reports that in recent months the response rate has been poor, possibly due to people’s fear of identity theft. Only three success rates have been reported for overseas mailshots (Canada to UK, UK to Canada, UK to USA), but they are all much lower, in the range 3-5%.

- Some people will reply with information but do not wish to continue the contact. You should, of course, not bother them again.
- Successive mailshots over a period may gradually increase the number of respondents, and your coverage of the bearers of the name. Over a period of five years successive mailshots for the Hempshall ONS have succeeded in establishing the places of 90% of living UK Hem(p)s(h)a/ells on the tree.
- Bear in mind that people definitely get “family-history mailshot fatigue” just as they do all sorts of other mailshot fatigue.

4.5.6 Benefits

- (Duncalf ONS) *“I sent out what became the first of my One-name newsletters (in 1984), and several of those who replied (some have unfortunately died since) are still subscribing to it today.”*
- It is worth the effort, even just for a few replies. Every little bit of information helps to fit another piece of the jigsaw, and potentially saves you £9.25 on buying a certificate.
- The one person who does respond may be the only family member who is keen on family history and can be very helpful, as was the case for the Attersley ONS.

So be bold and mail people! It has paid off for many Guild members – it can pay off for you too!

5. Responding to Enquiries

5.1 Guild requirements

All Guild registered members are required to respond to all enquiries made to them via email or reply-paid letters. It is important that Guild members with a registered study take this obligation seriously, as any failure to respond reflects on the Guild as a whole and may even impact on our charitable status, which requires us to provide benefits to the wider public.

Responding to enquiries Madeleine Jacob age 11

You may wish to have prepared some general background on your name to pass on, as well as any specific data in answer to the enquiry. You will certainly want to keep track of correspondents with some means of managing your email contacts (see *5:3: Managing your contacts list* below).

You may find it best not to pass back too much information, at least to begin with, so as to encourage your correspondents to give you what relevant information they may have about the name. You should also guard against others posting your entire trees into publicly available repositories such as the IGI. To minimise this risk, don't send massive GEDCOM files, but rather relevant extracts in the form of drop-line trees.

Remember that most correspondents won't be interested in your one-name study, but rather whether you can help them with their own family history.

5.2 Etiquette

Your research may sometimes put you in an ethical dilemma if you re-discover events in the past two or three generations that have been air-brushed out of the picture and are now unknown to the family concerned, for example:

- extramarital births
- adoptions
- bigamy
- criminal convictions

Many Guild Forum members are of the view that it is best to remain silent about these, since disclosure may perturb other people's lives. If you are approached by a member of a family that is not your own to "solve" such a mystery, you are allowed to politely avoid supplying information if you think doing so will avoid you appearing to take sides in a family row.

5.3 Managing your contacts list

If publicising your study has been successful, you should receive a number of enquiries about your study name, from a wide variety of people. It is obvious that your task of responding to them will be made much simpler if you can easily recall who the previous enquirers are, what their interest was, and what you have previously told them.

There are a variety of methods to keep track of the many contacts made through a one-name study, and for linking them to a genealogy database.

Many one-namers make an entry in their genealogy software package for each correspondent, and then link it either as a source record or a person record to the lineage (see *1.6.1: Systems of naming*, above). This allows a rapid assessment of how several contacts are related as the line goes backwards. However this system does not work well for contacts not yet associated with a lineage.

5.3.1 Software packages

There are many software solutions to the problem of keeping track of contacts, but it can be a challenge to find one that works the way you do.

- **Outlook** has a contacts section which suffices for some one-namers.
- **Goldmine** (http://www.goldmine.com) is a super-sized version of Outlook; it works very well to filter and group records when sending out mailings.
- **Microsoft Small Business Contact Manager** is an add-on for Outlook which allows one to keep track of contact history (dates, nature of contact etc.), but although it looks a useful facility for anyone running a FHS or a ONS to keep track of contacts and correspondence, there are no one-namers known to use it.
- **Kurlo** (http://www.kurlo.com) is a freeware contact manager (for Windows) with similar functionality, but again there are no reports of its use.
- **RGS-CardMaster** (http://users.belgacom.net/rgs/) is another freeware contact manager, with a card index/Rolodex style interface, address mailmerge with MS-Word, and an Inquiry Option to analyse almost anything. Simple to use but powerful if you need it. It is used in the Vousden ONS.
- **GenContacts** is (or was, as it appears not to be available any more) specialist software (Windows and Mac) produced by Family History Network. It used a relational database with multiple tables, and had functions for things such as Contacts, Contact History, Lineage, Records, Projects, and Subscriptions.
- If you have the relevant skills you can construct your own relational database, using suitable software such as **Access**, **OpenOffice.org Base** or **Filemaker Pro**;
- Simpler and perhaps just as effective is a 'flatfile' database in one of the above database programs or in a spreadsheet. A spreadsheet is quick to design and

develop into exactly what one wants, and to modify in the light of experience; it is also easy and fast to enter information and, most important, fast for searching.

- There are also online email systems which work effectively as contact managers, including **Gmail** (aka Googlemail) which works very well. This has the advantages that messages can be tagged in any way one wants (e.g. by lineage and/or by nature of task); a powerful search engine is supplied that will search the entire email archive; the need for back ups is eliminated; and groups of email addresses can be set up for mailings. Gmail also has the advantages that it has a very effective spam filter that removes the majority of spam from the inbox, and that the ONS contact list can be shared or handed over to someone else simply by giving them the password.

5.3.2 Data requirements

The range of information stored in a contacts list or database is, of course, a matter of personal preferences, but the following shows the structure of the Chandler one-name study contacts list (in Excel), and illustrates fields worth considering:

- REF NO – cross-referenced to every Vital Event connected with that contact in the database, and to the email folder for that contact – there may be more than one contact per Vital Event;
- CONTACT NAME – name in capitals followed by forename(s) followed by greeting name in brackets;
- ADDRESS – snail mail and/or email address;
- EARLIEST KNOWN ANCESTOR (EKA) – this is the current "brick wall" for that contact – forename(s) only except for variant surnames;
- DATE OF EKA – year followed by a letter (c for christening, b for burial, w for will, etc);
- COUNTY/STATE/PROVINCE. For static families, this is where the EKA lived. For migrating families, the common format GLS > HAM > NSW is used;
- PLACE – where the EKA lived, or the main settlement points for migrating families – often four or five place names entered;
- OTHER INFORMATION – any other notes, including brief conversation-helping notes about the contact, e.g. likes dogs, hates technology; but not sensitive personal comments;
- DATE OF MOST RECENT CONTACT – self-explanatory.

5.3.3 Paper-based solutions

If a paper-based approach is preferred, the actual contact details can be dealt with in a variety of ways.

- A lever-arch file with details of names, addresses and personal details, and even copies/printouts of correspondence.

- Index card, 5" x 3", which it has been suggested can be kept more conveniently on a 'Rolodex' system which has cards mounted likes spokes of a wheel on a spindle, making the cards much faster to locate than in a card-index box.

- A notebook with lineages coded and the same code repeated as computer folder names, email folders, in the filing cabinet and as a code in genealogy software. This enables an overview of the line to be made, with printouts of descendant summaries and a list of the contacts.

6. Publication of results

The Guild is very keen for its members to publish their work, in whatever form is appropriate. To encourage this, the Guild has run a number of annual competitions for essays and books, notably the 2009 Guild Publication Award which received over 100 entries. Starting in 2012, the Guild has instituted an annual "Guild Award of Excellence" for published works.

Publication of your one-name study serves several purposes. Not only is it advertising your achievement, but it is also creating a permanent record of your work which can survive you. In addition, by presenting your work in a readable form that recognises the value of the contributions you have received, and that will attract others to contribute more information, you will have had the opportunity and the incentive to review your research, revisit your data and perhaps obtain a fresh perspective on your study.

Last but not least, you will be repaying society for the free availability of church and administrative information, and for the generous advice and assistance of the many strangers who have helped you. It is even possible that your work could represent a significant contribution to the academic world in the fields of social history and demography.

There are many ways to publish and places to publish your study's results, including:

- The Guild's *Journal of One-Name Studies*
- Other genealogy magazines (do mention the Guild!)
- Your own One-Name Society journal (where applicable)
- One-off private one-name study books
- Booklets
- One-name study websites
- Guild profile pages
- Guild seminars
- One-name blogs
- Genuki
- Wikipedia

As in other branches of family history, some of the information gathered will be about living persons. Handling this information requires that you respect their privacy (see 6.4: Privacy of Living People, below). You should also be aware of copyright issues; advice and assistance on this can be obtained from various sources, such as the *Joint Guidelines on Copyright and Academic Research* published jointly by the British Academy and the Publishers Associations, April 2008 (http://www.britac.ac.uk/policy/joint-copyright-guide.cfm).

6.1 One-name study articles

The *Journal of One-Name Studies* published quarterly by the Guild has a wide selection of articles about members' own one-name studies, which are well worth reading. In 2006 the Guild produced a searchable CD entitled "*Celebrating 100 Guild Journals*", which contains all the Guild *Journal* articles from 1981 to 2006.

In addition, there are other essay-length accounts of members' one-name studies available on the Guild website, some of which were submitted as entries to the Guild's essay competitions, and others were produced as one of the elements of the Pharos Advanced Course in One-Name Studies.

6.2 One-name study books

Writing a book may seem a daunting task, but it can be a rewarding and effective way to document your research and pass it on to future generations. To get ideas on how to do this, look at what others have done – but remember, your research is unique and your book will be likewise. Write it with a view to the future, enabling you to update it easily, perhaps also to convert it to HTML for web purposes. For example, you might consider paginating the book on a chapter basis rather than as a continuous sequence of pages, which makes it easier to insert new material. Consider carefully whether to use colour: this will make the printing much more expensive.

The simplest method of getting material printed these days is to convert the final version to PDF. That way your publisher will have minimal work to do and the cost will therefore be minimised. Shop around for a publisher who can handle small print runs.

If you want to sell copies of your book, then don't put the same research on the web as well, or you will never sell the book! Some one-namers have found that they get much more feedback from people who read the book than they do from those who read a website. A very short print-run (e.g. 10) may be advisable at first, as no sooner have you published than people come out with more details to add to the book! However, this depends on having a publisher willing to do this. Some have found that, once the book is on the printer's system, quite small batches of further copies (e.g. 20 at a time) can be reprinted without any new set-up charge, but the set-up charge is quite large even if only minimal changes are made.

Several Guild members have found that the publishing facilities offered by firms such as Lulu (http://www.lulu.com) are ideal for their purpose, since this provides a print-to-order facility. Instead of using a standard publisher and ordering a print run of a hundred or so copies, with Lulu you simply upload a PDF copy of your book to their website to add it to their online catalogue. Then anyone who wants to buy a copy of your book can order it from Lulu and a copy is individually printed for them. The cost of the book can even be cheaper than for a small conventional print run, and you don't have to estimate in advance how many copies to print and sell. You can set a price for the book and either just cover your publishing cost or even make a small profit on each copy. Even better, you can update your book as many times as you wish simply by uploading a new revised version.

Examples are given here of different approaches to the content of the book. See also 6.2.1: ONS books published by Guild members, below.

The Jephcott ONS book

This book was written in the 1990s and by 2007 reached its fourth edition. It turned out to be 1000 pages of A4 size, weighing 3kg, and costing £70 each plus postage. About 40 were sold.

The structure is:

1. Introductory Section
2. The Jephcott Name – a description of the etymology of the name and its many variants
3. The Jephcott Society – information about the society
4. Heraldry
5. Parish Records
6. Family Tree Collection – this is the big one. It forms over half of the book, broken down into about 50 lines of descent that it has not been possible to connect up. Each family includes trees, letters, pictures, etc.
7. Demographic Studies – maps of surname dispersal, etc.
8. Census Records
9. Genealogical Indexes – Boyds, various card index references, etc.
10. Births at the GRO – full index of all references found 1837 to c1920
11. Marriages at the GRO – ditto
12. Deaths at the GRO – ditto
13. Wills and Administrations
14. Monumental Inscriptions
15. Freemen of the City and Apprenticeship Records
16. University Graduates and Scholars
17. Army, Navy and Air Force Records
18. Taxation, Law and Order – hearth tax, settlement certs, ne'er-do-wells, etc.
19. Trade and Telephone Directories – Kelly's etc.
20. Newspapers and other Publications
21. Miscellaneous Sources
22. Reference

The Hempsall ONS book

The Hempsalls ONS book was published in 2006 and runs to 200 pages of A4. It sells for £24, with discounts for multiple copies. It has more than paid for all the research and has even made a modest profit. About 130 copies have been sold in the UK, and a further 60 or so in North America and Australia. This compares to a world-wide population of about 650 Hempsalls, and 400 or so other variants (which are dealt with less thoroughly in the book). Clearly, some buy one copy for a whole family, others aren't interested, others haven't yet been contacted or haven't contacted the author. A lot of purchasers are female line relatives, some several steps away from the male name. Smaller in size than the Jephcott book, this does not include full lists from censuses, BMDs etc. It is nearly all continuous text, rather than lists and records which are available elsewhere. It does however include full transcripts of most pre 1858 wills, excluding less interesting ones. The chapters are as follows:

1. Foreword
2. Table of contents
3. Chapter One: Distribution of HEMPSALLs
4. Chapter Two: Earliest Records of HEMPSALLs and Similar Name Spellings
5. Chapter Three: Nottinghamshire HEMPSALLs in the 17th Century
6. Chapter Four: HEMPSALLs in the 18th Century
7. Chapter Five: HEMPSALLs in the Nineteenth Century
8. Chapter Six: HEMPSALLs in the Twentieth Century
9. Appendix A: HEMPSALL family Outline Descendant Tree
10. Appendix B: Photographs

The descendant tree, which fortunately links nearly all known lines with the various name variants, enables any enquirer who knows an ancestor alive in 1901 to be able to trace their ancestry back to about 1540. This section is in 8-point type face to cram as much in as possible, incorporating BMDs, places etc.

6.2.1 ONS books published by Guild members

The Guild Wiki gives a full list of one-name study books published by Guild members. The following is a list of those available for loan via the Guild library scheme and hence included as such in the Online Library Catalogue on the Guild website. Most are available in printed book form; a few are available as CDs or DVDs.

- Bob Alderman: *The Alderman One-Name Project*.
- Bob Alderman, Mari Alderman and Neil Alderman: *Early Alderman Wills in Northamptonshire (1522-1858)*. Privately printed, 2008, 228 pages.
- Wendy Angove: *The Jigsaw Puzzle Tree*. Privately printed, 304 pages.
- David Austerberry: *The Austerberry Saga*. Privately printed, 2007, 156 pages.
- Peter Badham: *Badham Delvings*. Privately printed, 2007, 240 pages.
- J.W. Blencowe: *The Blencowe Families of Cumbria and Northamptonshire and their descendants*.
- Joy Gann Brown: *The Ganns 1200 – 1800 AD: A journey of 600 years and 6000 miles*.
- Robert Bruce Cathcart: *Cathcart in Australia*. Privately printed, 1998, 202 pages.
- Peter Crabtree: *Crabtree: Dweller by the Wild Apple Tree*, privately printed, 2004, 334 pages.
- Sheila Fermor Clarkson: *Over Half a Century of Fermor Family Cricket: Part 2, 1946*.
- Michael Dummer: *The Family of Dummer of British Origin*.
- Jean Getchell: *Donisthorpes in England and the United States*.
- John Reid Hebden: *Sir John Hebdon Kt 1612-1670: His history and family*.
- David Heppenstall Mellor: *Born Hep or Born to be Hep*.
- The Metcalfe Society: *Metcalfe: History of the Clan*. Privately printed, 2000, 252 pages.
- D Meredith McFadden: *Salt and Silk: Chronicles of the Aubreys of Clehonger, a Herefordshire family*. Aubrey Warsash Publications, 2005, 242 pages.
- Alex J McGahey: *The Saga of the Beckinghams and Kaiser Bill (1914-1919)*. Privately printed, 2002.
- Donald McIlhagga: *McIlhagga Clan History*.
- Teresa and Stuart Pask. *Pasks of Lincolnshire. Volume I: Great Gonerby*.
- Estella Yule Pryor: *The Yule Families of Kincardineshire, Scotland*. Privately printed 2008, 234 pages.
- Estella Yule Pryor: *The Yule Families of Northeast Aberdeenshire (Fraserburgh, Rathen and Strichen), Scotland*. Privately printed, 2009, 240 pages.

- Estella Yule Pryor: *The Yule Families of Buchan (Lonmay, Crimond, Peterhead, Cruden etc.), Aberdeenshire, Scotland.* Privately printed 2009, 276 pages.
- Estella Yule Prior: *The Yule Families of Western Aberdeenshire, Scotland.* Privately printed, 2008, 198 pages.
- Dawn Raimondo (or Dawn Stapylton-Adkins): *Soldiers, Shoemakers and Simons Town: The story of the Brewitt Family.* Privately printed, 2005, 176 pages.
- Alan Savin: *The Savin Sagas.*
- Betty Choyce Sheehan: *The Choice / Choyce Compendium.* Privately printed, 2006, 1076 pages.
- Glenda Thornton: *Dead Relatives: The Rise and Fall of the Phillibrowns.*
- Vicky Uffindell: *The Uffindell Family Vol.1 : Fenland Farmers of Haddenham, Cambs., and their Compositor Cousins.* Uffindell Books, 2003, 300 pages.
- Colin Ulph: *Ulph Family History.* Privately printed, 2005.
- Oscar De Ville: *A Miscellany of Articles on The Medieval Deyville Family.* Privately printed, 2005, pp222.
- Antony Turner Widgery: *Samuel and Mary Widgery, A Devon Family in North America.*
- Ann Williams: *The Astridge Family Roll of Honour.*

6.2.2 Genealogy-related books published by Guild members

In addition to the list of one-name study books, there is a page on the Guild Wiki giving a list of genealogy-related books published by Guild members.

6.2.3 General notes on publishing a book

Formal publications should use an ISBN/ISSN and copies should be deposited in the copyright libraries. (Booksellers are unlikely to sell your book if it does not have an ISBN.) If your published book has an ISBN number you should register with the Public Lending Right (PLR) and the Authors' Licensing and Collecting Society (ALCS) so that you receive royalty payments when your book is borrowed or photocopied. There is further information on the PLR and ALCS in the Members' Room (http://www.one-name.org/members/PLR_ALCS.html). If you have received a contract to publish a book you should consider joining the Society of Authors (http://www.societyofauthors.net) who will offer advice on contracts, copyright and other related matters.

6.3 One-name study websites

A one-name study website is an excellent way to publish your results, as it is easy to update as new information is found. It also maximises the chance of others finding your study, and thus combines *publishing* your study with *publicising* your study! Members report that they get more contacts through their website than any other source, including the Guild itself.

Even if you don't have a website, do think about creating a Guild profile page, which is really easy to do.

The following advice on what makes a good website is taken from the judging criteria for the Guild's website competitions which were run for many years in the past. More advice can also be found in Teresa Pask's presentation on *Creating a One-Name Study Website* which is included in the Guild website's Seminar section at http://www.one-name.org/members/seminars.html.

6.3.1 Criteria for a one-name website

The website should display good design, easy and logical navigation, technical compliance with web standards and informative, worldwide, one-name content.

Basic criteria

- The initial page should be reasonably quick to download. Web users are often impatient and, if a page takes a long time to appear, they will lose patience and look elsewhere.
- Images, which take longer to download, should be used to good effect but not overdone, and their size should not be excessive.
- The initial page should be attractive and welcoming in appearance. First impressions are all important and, having got visitors, you want to persuade them to stay.
- Don't overload pages with information: a clean look with plenty of "white space" is to be preferred.
- Navigation around the site should be easy and consistently presented. Allow visitors to progress through your site without forcing them back to the main menu every time.
- Ensure that the text can be read easily and that text and background colours do not clash. Don't use fonts that others won't have installed on their systems.
- Avoid "pop-ups" and advertising banners that may detract from the message you want to convey.
- The title and initial text should convey clearly to visitors that it is a One-Name website and inform them about the sort of information they will find on the site. It should entice them to explore further.
- The website should be neat and logically presented, to reflect the fact that your information has been researched and is presented in a similar fashion.
- Ensure that there are no errors in spelling or grammar. Such errors may give the impression that the information in the rest of the site could be unreliable.
- Do provide an overall site index or map.
- Choose a short, meaningful, URL for the site.
- When designing the page layout, remember that visitors will be using a range of different screen resolutions from 800 x 600, through the popular 1024 x 768, up to the larger sizes found on modern flat screen displays, such as 1280 x 1024. Many new computers are now using 'wide-screen' displays. Users will find it irritating if they have to continually scroll their browser window sideways to view a page. Avoid fixed size 'wallpapers' which are often optimized for a single screen size.
- Browsers can sometimes differ in the way they display pages, especially if you are using Javascript. You should make sure that all your web pages appear correctly with a range of modern browsers, such as MS Internet Explorer, Firefox, Safari, Google Chrome, and Opera.
- Do validate the coding on your pages, using sites such as http://validator.w3.org.

One-Name content

Visitors to a website devoted to a surname are usually interested in general information about the surname itself. A one-name study website should include such information as:

- What is the meaning of the surname?
- What are the recognised spelling variants?
- What is its origin and how is it distributed?

- How has the distribution changed over time? What are the patterns of immigration and emigration? (Remember that your study is worldwide, so reflect that in your content).
- Are there any famous or newsworthy people with the surname, either currently or in history? If so, what information is there about them?
- Have any grants of arms been made to people with the surname? If so, is there a description either in words (the blazon) or as an image (the emblazon)?
- Are there any other websites devoted to the surname or with information? If so are links provided to visit?
- Are there any Mailing Lists, Forums, Message Boards, Blogs, Newsfeeds, DNA studies etc. in existence for the surname? If so, are details and/or links provided?
- Photographs can enhance the site, but ensure they don't slow it down.
- Ensure that there is a link to the Guild's website and that your site is listed on the Guild page for your study.
- Provide details of co-researchers on your study, or details of your One-Name society.

Data on individuals

The amount of information about specific individuals provided on websites will differ. Some may include source data only, some may include reconstructed family groups, some may include both. Some may even display complete pedigrees.

Contact information

In all cases, the site should make it clear how you can be contacted and what information should be provided for any query.

6.3.2 Creating a website

You will obviously need some web space; check whether your ISP provides some for free. If so, you might find that you can access it using a URL like this:

http://webpages.yourisp.com/~yourname/

but for a small cost you may be able to have your own domain name such as:

http://www.yourname.name or http://www.yourname.info

which do sound rather better and more professional. (But avoid .com or .co.uk domain names as these imply a commercial website.)

There are very many companies selling web space with varying levels of functionality and at varying prices. Some of them may provide an "easy web" facility for creating the web site without needing to have technological expertise on HTML, etc.; alternatively you might prefer to investigate the web editor programs shown below.

You will also need an FTP program to upload the pages to your web space. Many Windows users find that Windows Explorer is adequate for this, but you might prefer to download and install one of the many free FTP programs.

Designing your website

You will need to consider the design of your website. What pages are you going to have? How should the user move from page to page? Design the page template and navigation, and make sure that every page follows it. Keep the design criteria in *6.3.1: Criteria for a one-name website* in mind throughout.

Do look at previous Guild Web Award winners for ideas.

The home page

First impressions are important: make the first page (the home page) quick to load. Make sure this page introduces the website and explains what's in it. It should make it clear that it's about a one-name study - not your family history.

Page design

Create a consistent style and structure for colours, text, menus and navigation. A consistently presented 'navigation bar' ('navbar') is ideal. If you can learn to use CSS stylesheets this will help maintain your style.

Make sure your page is listed on the Guild's Register database.

6.3.2.1 Web publishing software programs

It is quite possible to build your website using nothing more elaborate than a plain text editor such as Wordpad or Notepad – but this can be quite hard work. Instead there are a range of different options for building your website, from the ultra-simple (and free) to the professional-level (and expensive). The following gives a sample of what is available.

Many **ISPs** offer an "easy website builder" package (under a variety of names) for creating a website, sometimes limited to a given number of pages according to the webhosting package you have chosen. These are normally based on customisable templates for a range of typical applications and claim to take no more than 5 or 10 minutes to generate a website!

Many **genealogy programs** can automatically produce web pages from their databases. Some examples of packages that do this are (beware of confusion between the first two, similarly named, packages on the list!):

- **The Master Genealogist (TMG) and Second Site** (http://ss.johncardinal.com). TMG is very widely used for genealogy and one-name studies, and Second Site is a genealogy web site builder designed for use with TMG, in order to publish TMG data in HTML format. In fact, Second Site provide a complete website service since it also integrates closely with the Family History Hosting ISP to provide hosting services as well.

- **The Next Generation (TNG) of Genealogy Sitebuilding** (http://www.tngsite-building.com) TNG takes almost the other extreme, in that rather than convert your PC's genealogy data into a website, the TNG genealogy package runs on a website using a MySQL database and PHP scripting. The pages of the website are generated on-the-fly from the database rather than being static snapshots of the data held. Extensive help is provided in getting a web hosting package with the required facilities.

- **Family Historian** (www.family-historian.co.uk/) is a genealogy software program with in-built wizards for generating family tree websites.

- There are also utilities that can convert a Gedcom file to static web pages - see Cyndi's List www.cyndislist.com/gedcom.htm#HTML.

Dreamweaver is the program used by the professionals. It has a steep learning curve but editing in WYSIWYG ("What You See Is What You Get") makes it very user friendly – no need to learn how to code. It is expensive to buy (around £400). Very few family history websites will require this degree of sophistication. There is a Student and Teacher Edition which can be bought on Amazon for around £100-£125, but there are strict qualifying criteria and the program is only licensed for use on one computer. Dreamweaver is used to maintain and develop the Society of Genealogists' website. The Pask (http://pask.org.uk/) and Uridge (http://uridge.org/) websites were largely created using Dreamweaver.

FrontPage was included with some (early) versions of Microsoft Office. It has a reputation for producing bloated code which is difficult to edit, but it is used by many people who find that it is easy to use and to integrate with other Microsoft applications. FrontPage was discontinued in late 2006 to be replaced by Microsoft Expression Web. FrontPage was used to create the Sherwood ONS website (http://www.sherwoodfam.plus.com/) .

Originally produced by Allaire, **Macromedia Homesite** is a well-featured web-editor without the complexity of Dreamweaver (see above). Macromedia was taken over by Adobe and the program is no longer being developed, though it may still be available. The program was used to create the Hollyer Family Website (http://www.hollyer.info).

Nvu (pronounced N-view) is a basic free web authoring system which is available in versions for Microsoft Windows, Linux and Apple Mac. Nvu (which stands for "new view") has an inbuilt FTP (file transfer protocol) program and is very easy to use. The WYSYWIG doesn't create bloated code and can be edited manually if necessary.

6.4 One-name blogs

One-name blogs are easy to create by utilising a free blogging program such as Google Blogger or Wordpress. See Blogfinder (http://blogfinder.genealogue.com) for a list of single-surname blogs. Cyndi's List has a useful page on blogs which explains the basic terminology and provides guidance on using and subscribing to blogs.

There is a page on the Guild Wiki listing the one-name blogs run by Guild members.

6.5 Privacy of living people

There are differing opinions about how information relating to living people should be handled; some one-namers believe that it should never be published or distributed without the permission of each person concerned, some believe that it can be distributed if it is in the public domain (e.g. GRO Indexes, or matters described in a newspaper article). In the former case this effectively means you should not publish any information about persons born within the past 100 years unless they have given specific approval, or unless you are certain that they are no longer alive.

Any publication or information sent to others should respect the laws of the relevant country or countries. In the UK this means the Data Protection Act. There are many misconceptions about what this legislation does and does not allow, and it is worth reading the summary of the situation that the Guild received a decade ago, which clearly states what limitations are placed on the use of personal data. This position appears to have been updated since the 1998 UK Data Protection Act came into effect.

In particular, it has been claimed that it is illegal to publish trees on the Internet which include details of any living person, unless you have their express permission, but this is not true. People have the right to have information about themselves removed or corrected, but you don't require prior permission to publish it — or newspapers would go out of business, and popstars would have undisturbed private lives. Ancestry have published the GRO index entries relating to millions of births, marriages and deaths, but they have not asked the permission of each individual to do so, though it appears that in principle one could get entries relating to oneself removed.

On the other hand it is good ethical practice for genealogists not to publish details of the living without permission, and in this respect the US National Genealogical Society's Genealogical Standards and Guidelines: Standards For Sharing Information With Others are particularly relevant (and they have been endorsed by the Society of Genealogists).

This is a fairly contentious subject and the NGS Guidelines are thought by some to be less to do with ethics than the paranoia associated with potential litigation.

6.5.1 1998 Data Protection Act

An exchange of emails on the 1998 UK Data Protection Act between Guild member Chris Pomery and the Office of the Information Commissioner, in 2002 and 2007, confirms that family historians are not only not required to register, we are not even required to follow the eight principles of data protection outlined in the 1998 Act.

Part of the confusion has arisen because under the previous Act of 1984 genealogists were exempted provided that they did not disclose personal data to third parties. Section 36 of the 1998 Act extends this principle and removes the proviso. But it also reminds us that we should use the data we gather only for the purposes for which we need it and that we should remain sensitive to how others may feel about our holding and using it. It even opens up the possibility that case law may cause this situation to be reviewed in future regardless of the advice received from the OIC.

7. Preserving your study

Most Guild members put in an enormous amount of time and energy on their one-name studies. It is essential that this investment is protected and preserved – i.e. that it is both protected against day-to-day dangers, and preserved for the future.

You should seek to preserve and archive your work during your lifetime and make arrangements for its preservation after you die.

7.1 Safeguarding your study

You should consider the kind of hazards that your study may be subject to, and the consequences should any of them come to pass. These can range from accidentally deleting or corrupting a file through "finger trouble", to loss of your entire data due to disk or computer failure, or even loss of your computer and all your data through fire or theft.

Members therefore need to take steps to safeguard their studies from day to day by ensuring that critical data is backed up in multiple ways and locations. An important and easy-to-remember preservation principle developed at Stanford University is **LOCKSS** (**L**ots **O**f **C**opies **K**eep **S**tuff **S**afe). The basic concept is that the more copies you archive in different locations, the safer your records will be.

Thus you might decide to have backups of your data held locally, where the data is easily accessible for update or refresh, plus archive copies of the same data (perhaps rather older) held in one or more remote locations.

7.1.1 Backups

Backups are intended to enable a study to be recovered should something go wrong, such as accidental deletion or corruption of a single record, or a hard-disk failure, or loss of a laptop computer.

There are several ways of backing up your data, from simply copying files by hand to another medium or – preferably – using one of the specialist software packages such as Acronis (http://www.acronis.co.uk) or SmartSync (http://www.smartsync.com). The best of such packages take only a few minutes to update the backup with just the files that have changed since the last backup, making the whole process easy, quick, and potentially fully automatic.

The ease and speed of the backup is important, since backups should be carried out frequently. This is especially true when sufficient data has been added since the previous backup for the new data not to be easily reconstituted – or, indeed, reconstituted at all – from the original sources. If an automatic process is being used, then it is possible to have backups being taken continually as you work; alternatively, you could choose to have the backup refreshed at the end of each working day.

Whatever the frequency chosen, you should also reckon to have several "generations" of backup available to you; for instance, you may have a set of external backup media that are maintained with the data as it was yesterday, a week ago, a month ago, and a year ago. This could be important: if the backup you take today contains errors, then you may have lost the "good" backup you had previously and you may need to resort to one of your older backups to recover your data.

It need hardly be said that you should also ensure that your backups are regularly verified so that you are confident that the files can be restored if needed. For this reason a backup package that just copies your files rather than encoding or compressing the data in its own format is preferable to, say, Norton Ghost or similar products.

7.1.1.1 Backup methods

There are various methods of backing up data both online and offline. To safeguard your data against all eventualities it is wise to back up your files in multiple locations. If you collaborate with other researchers, consider exchanging key files for offsite backup.

External hard drives

External hard drives can be purchased for a relatively small sum of money and provide a useful means of backing up files onsite. Files can be backed up manually or the process can be automated using special software such as Acronis (http://www.acronis.co.uk/).

Note that:

- Backing up onto an external hard disk which is permanently plugged into the computer will normally give protection against failure of the computer's internal hard disc and against accidental deletion or editing of records. It is unlikely to give protection against fire or theft.

- Backing up onto an external hard disc which is then removed from the premises (e.g. taken into work) should give protection against fire, theft, accidental deletion, internal hard-disc failure. The act of backing-up will necessitate bringing the hard disc to the computer, at least overnight, so there will be a slight risk that the backup and the original will both be lost because of a fire or theft during this period.

- Backing up on to an external website is the most secure method, but can be time-consuming since upload speeds are generally much slower than download speeds. Backing up needs to be to a password-protected folder.

DVDs, CDs, USB memory sticks

Memory sticks, flash drives or thumb drives can be useful media for backups, but may not be reliable or robust enough to depend on.

CDs or DVDs can provide a useful write-once backup medium, and as such are more suitable for archives than for backups (which typically get refreshed regularly). If a home-written CD or DVD is required for long-term storage of archive data, then a high-quality disk is needed; you can buy "gold" or "archival quality" CDs and DVDs which are recommended for this purpose. Once written, keep the disks cool and away from light sources.

Online storage

There are now many companies which provide online storage in "the cloud". This is a very secure method of backing up files, in that the data is unaffected by any damage or loss to the original data or computer, but the user should be wary of relying entirely on one provider. If a company ceases trading there is no guarantee that your data will be preserved. Most companies will offer a few gigabytes of storage free of charge, but a monthly or annual subscription is required if additional storage is needed. Some companies will offer chunks of extra storage or credit if you recommend the service to your friends.

Backup services use your computer's idle time and the upload part of a broadband subscription – "set it and forget it". The initial process can be time-consuming since upload speeds are generally much slower than download speeds. Backing up needs to be to a password-protected folder. You can also download your own backup to a different computer or in a different location, if you so wish. Some of the services will also retain a version history.

- **Adrive** (http://www.adrive.com) – 50 Gb of free online storage
- **Amazon Cloud Drive** (http://www.amazon.com/cloudddrive/learnmore) – 5 Gb of free online storage
- **BackBlaze** (http://www.backblaze.com) – online backup service offering unlimited storage for $5 per month or $50 per year
- **Boxnet** (http://www.box.net) – 5 Gb of free online storage
- **Carbonite** (http://www.carbonite.com) is a US-based service which offers unlimited online backup for a flat fee of $59 per year
- **Cloudme** (http://www.cloudme.com) – 3 Gb of free online storage
- **Dropbox** (http://www.dropbox.com) – 2 Gb of free online storage. You gain an extra 250 Mb of storage for each friend who joins.
- **Mediafire** (http://www.mediafire.com) – a free service supported by advertising
- **Mozy** (http://mozy.co.uk) – the first 2Gb of storage space is free to personal users
- **SugarSync** (http://www.sugarsync.com) has a number of paid-for plans including a 5Gb plan (which is not a trial but a free account)
- **Trend Micro SafeSync** (http://tinyurl.com/7hqv4by) – a UK-based remote backup service

Services such as **GoogleDocs** (http://docs.google.com) and **Windows Live Skydrive** (http://explore.live.com/windows-live-skydrive) are primarily designed for collaborative working but can also be used to store files online. GoogleDocs provides one gigabyte of free storage and accepts a variety of file formats including GEDCOM files. Windows Live Skydrive provides 25 gigabytes of free storage but is designed to work with Microsoft file formats and photos and might not accept all file formats.

Paper

Computers are not safe storage places. If the information is vital then keep hard copies as well. There is a danger that if we solely back up data digitally a situation could arise in the future where the data cannot be read. This is less of an issue in an active study where the archives have been upgraded as the technology evolves, but has implications in a lapsed study. Paper files should be stored on acid-free paper or parchment.

Further reading

FamilySearch have produced an interesting *White Paper* on the subject of *Preserving your Family History Records Digitally*, by Gary T Wright, available on the FamilySearch Wiki at http://wiki.familysearch.org/en/White_Paper:_Preserving_Your_Family_History_Records_Digitally

7.2 Archiving your study

7.2.1 Your own archive copies

It is wise to keep your own archives of your work, perhaps by retaining backup media such as CDs or DVDs, especially if these are held off-site somewhere.

7.2.2 The Guild Electronic Archive

Members are encouraged to use the facilities available on the Guild website – the surname "Archive" pages – to hold their one-name study data in a form that not only holds it safely but also makes it searchable.

At launch, the Guild Electronic Archive supported the storage of records of indexes for Births, Marriages and Deaths from the General Register Offices in England and Wales and for Scotland, together with Adoptions recorded in England and Wales, and census and civil probate records.

This has since been extended to allow users the opportunity to define their own sets of records, structured according to the needs of their individual one-name study. User-defined record sets operate in the same way as the system defined record sets, such as Birth, Marriage and Death records, but are tailored according to the needs of the individual archivist. Record sets can be defined to support any set of records held relating to a one-name study; for example Apprenticeships, Directorships, Irish records – there is no limit to the number and type of record sets that may be defined. The archivist can even define non-standard record sets for system defined records if it is wished to structure them differently from those defined by the archive.

The data (in the required text format) can be easily uploaded at any time to the archive on the Guild website.

A one-name study archive on the Guild website can operate in any of four modes:

- **Open**. The contents of the archive are accessible from the public area of the Guild website, and appropriate links to access it may also be placed on a member's website.

- **Registered**. The contents of the archive are accessible from the public area of the Guild website by those members of the public who have registered with your archive.
- **Restricted**. The contents of the archive may be accessed only from the Members' room of the Guild web site by fellow members of the Guild.
- **Advertised**. The contents of the archive may be accessed only from the Members' room of the Guild website by fellow members of the Guild, though the existence of the archive is advertised to members of the public.

At all times the data remains the property of the Guild member, who is encouraged to define what should happen to the archive in the event of his leaving the Guild or of his demise. Many members choose to use the archive facility as a means of storing records with the Guild for access by members or by the public after their own death.

7.2.3 Lodging material with the Guild Library

The Guild encourages its members to document their one-name studies and deposit copies with appropriate organisations, e.g. The Society of Genealogists, County Record Offices, or Local Studies Centres. The reasons for doing this include not only making the results of your study available to a wider audience, but also providing a secure off-site location for the information you have collected.

The Society of Genealogists in London boxes unpublished family histories received in paper form. It welcomes such deposits but has rules of its own about what is acceptable; see the leaflet http://www.sog.org.uk/leaflets/depositresearch.pdf. The catalogue to its surname collections is available online at http://www.sog.org.uk/library/surnames.shtml.

The LDS Family History Library in Salt Lake City, Utah also accepts deposits of surname material for long-term preservation .

The Guild itself is happy to receive your archived work but prefers this to be in digital format on CD or DVD, as we have no premises suitable for storage of significant amounts of physical material. Details of how this material should be presented are given on the page *Lodging ONS material with the Guild* at http://www.one-name.org/members/donating.html.

If you are depositing such a CD or DVD with the Guild Library, you should also indicate the basis on which it is being lodged, e.g.

- "The Guild may distribute this information now to anyone that is interested in my registered name", or
- "Should I cease to be a member, the Guild may release the information on this disc in whole or in part to anyone interested in my registered name" , or
- "Should I cease to be a Guild member this disc should be destroyed or returned to me".

7.2.4 Submitting material to the Guild Online Library

Material submitted to the Guild Library as described in the section above will be held for safekeeping but will not be published. From the point of view of permitting access to one-name study data, it is better to submit the archive to the Guild's Online Library, where it can be made available to the membership.

The Online Library consists of a large number of files of various types held on the Guild website and accessed through the Online Library Catalogue in the Members' Room. The Catalogue can be searched for material relating to a specific surname or material of a specific type. Most files are indexed for searching, and a Google-type search is provided. All files are available for download.

To submit one-name study material to the Guild Online Library, contact the Webmaster.

7.3 Bequeathing your study

Maybe a melancholy subject, but we should consider what is to happen to our studies when we die, and make sure that our wishes are known.

Guild members are encouraged to fill in the form available in the "Self-Service" section of the Members Room, on "Preserving your study". This allows you to specify the following regarding the future of your study material:

- **Contact**: The individual whom the Guild should contact regarding your study material following notification of your death
- **Bequest**: A brief description of what is to happen to your study material upon your death.
- **Genealogical next-of-kin**: An individual who you believe might wish to take over your study following your death.

In addition, members can say what should happen to their Profile and Archive pages when they are no longer Guild members. The default, if no indication is given, is for both Profile and Archive pages to be deleted., You may however choose to leave these on the Guild website (with, of course, your contact details removed) for the benefit of future enquirers or of someone else taking over your registered study.

Attention is also drawn to the Will Codicil (http://www.one-name.org/members/willcodicil. html) suggested for use by Guild members wishing to include directions for their study materials in their Will.

7.4 Setting up a One-Name Society

The ultimate way of ensuring that your study continues after your death is to set up a Society which will carry it on. While it is a tough initial task to set up a one-name society, and relatively few Guild members have done so, I have yet to meet anyone who has done so who thinks it was a mistake or that running one is not worth the effort required.

Among the key potential benefits are:

- a regular income stream from annual or periodic subscriptions.
- an identified pool of researchers who can help you move your one-name study forward.
- a pool of volunteers to share the workload of running the society and the project.
- a good way to bring overseas researchers into the fold.

An effective way to set up a Society is to launch it at the close of a major event such as a reunion. At that point everyone is enthusiastic and in one place, two conditions that make signing them up much easier to achieve.

Running a One-Name Society

There are as many ways of running a Society as the Societies that actually exist. A key issue is how you communicate with your members. In the past the preferred way was to produce a newsletter or journal, and many members still produce and post physical copies to their members around the world. Many more produce a newsletter but in PDF format which just needs to be emailed to members. Another option is to switch these activities online, substituting a blog for the newsletter and a website for the journal.

Appendix: A One-Name Study Plan

Having read this Wiki Book you may want to consider how you can go about organising your own one-name study. This will depend on a number of factors, such as your own preferences and interests; your location; the distribution of your study name; current progress on your study; and the amount of time you have available. No two studies are the same, so there is no right way to start to carry out your study.

Having established the frequency of your name, you will want to decide whether to record your data manually or by using a combination of different computer programs (databases, spreadsheets, and/or genealogical programs). When organising your one-name study it is vitally important to keep a record of what data sources you have searched and the results found (including nil results), so as to maximise the efficiency of your data collection and minimise unproductive repeat searches.

A typical one-name study may be structured along the lines given in the following table. This list ensures that the main sources of data are collected first, followed by other data sources; it also leads on to the analysis and synthesis of your data, and hopefully to the eventual publication of your study.

Stage	Suggested activities for a one-name study plan
1	Identification of the frequency and distribution of the surname
Data collection	
2	Collect initial data on births, marriages and deaths
3	Collect all references in the International Genealogical Index (referring back to original records at a later date)
4	Search all available census records or census substitutes such as electoral rolls, starting on the most recent and working backwards
5	Collect all entries from major published Will indexes
6	Search available marriage indexes
7	Collect all burial records
8	Collect Monumental Inscriptions
9	Stages 2 to 8 will be undertaken for your main country (probably where you live). Repeat the data collection activities for all other countries where your study name exists.
10	Examine other major sources of data, initially concentrating your efforts on indexed sources and in the areas that will give the most returns
11	Examine original records such as parish records of baptisms, marriages and burials
12	Repeat stages 10 and 11 for all other countries where your study name exists
13	Submit your one-name study data to the Guild Marriage Index, Guild Scottish Index, and Guild Probate Index as appropriate, to assist other members in finding connections
14	Request searches from the Guild Marriage Challenges as they are offered
15	Use the Guild Marriage Index and/or Marriage Locator to identify the location of marriages
Data analysis	
16	Undertake family reconstructions using the data collected (this is unlikely to be feasible for large one-name studies)
17	Analyse the distribution and relative frequency of your study name in different places and across time
18	Analyse the distribution patterns for different name variants
19	Analyse missing data (such as a marriage church) to see if the data can be found
20	Consider setting up a DNA project to connect family groups and prove the connections between name variants
Data synthesis	
21	Assess the possible meaning of your study name
22	Assess the origin of the study name based on distribution and migration analysis
23	Identify how and where name variants arose
24	Identify the main patterns of distribution change, including emigration and immigration
25	See what other conclusions can be drawn from your data - such as longevity, infant mortality, number of pregnancies, social conditions, impact of extended families, changes in death rates over time
Store your data	
26	Consider how you want to store your one-name study data: manually or on a computer
27	Design your data structure to organise your data - see *JOONS*, October 2008, Vol.9 No.12 p.10, *Digitisation for One-Namers*, to see an example of a data structure
Publicise your one-name study	
28	Consider publicising your one-name study in as many places as possible
29	Consider creating a website or blog for your one-name study
30	As a minimum, use the Guild's Profile facility to help you get online
Publishing your one-name study	
31	Write articles about your study for the Guild *Journal* and other genealogy magazines
32	Consider writing your own ONS Newsletter, perhaps as part of a one-name Society
33	Consider writing a book on your one-name study
Safeguard and preserve your one-name study	
34	Routinely back up your one-name study data
35	Consider digitising all essential paper material from your one-name study
36	Consider depositing copies of your one-name study with appropriate organisations
37	Make arrangements for the preservation of your one-name study for when you are no longer able to continue your research work or when you die